T0286786

Cambridge Elements ≡

Elements in Religion and Monotheism
edited by
Paul K. Moser
Loyola University Chicago
Chad Meister
Bethel University

MONOTHEISM, SUFFERING, AND EVIL

Michael L. Peterson
Asbury Theological Seminary

CAMBRIDGE
UNIVERSITY PRESS

CAMBRIDGE
UNIVERSITY PRESS

University Printing House, Cambridge CB2 8BS, United Kingdom

One Liberty Plaza, 20th Floor, New York, NY 10006, USA

477 Williamstown Road, Port Melbourne, VIC 3207, Australia

314–321, 3rd Floor, Plot 3, Splendor Forum, Jasola District Centre,
New Delhi – 110025, India

103 Penang Road, #05–06/07, Visioncrest Commercial, Singapore 238467

Cambridge University Press is part of the University of Cambridge.

It furthers the University's mission by disseminating knowledge in the pursuit of
education, learning, and research at the highest international levels of excellence.

www.cambridge.org
Information on this title: www.cambridge.org/9781108822879
DOI: 10.1017/9781108906487

First published 2022

A catalogue record for this publication is available from the British Library.

ISBN 978-1-108-82287-9 Paperback
ISSN 2631-3014 (online)
ISSN 2631-3006 (print)

Monotheism, Suffering, and Evil

Elements in Religion and Monotheism

DOI: 10.1017/9781108906487
First published online: April 2022

Michael L. Peterson
Asbury Theological Seminary

Author for correspondence: Michael L. Peterson, mike.peterson@asburyseminary.edu

Abstract: Suffering and evil in the world provide the basis for the most difficult challenge to monotheistic belief. This Element discusses how the three great monotheisms – Judaism, Christianity, and Islam – respond to the problem of suffering and evil. Different versions of the problem, types of answers, and recurring themes in philosophical and religious sources are analyzed. Objections to the enterprise of theodicy are also discussed as are additional objections to the monotheistic God more broadly. This treatment culminates in a recommendation for how monotheism can best respond to the most serious formulation of the problem, the argument from gratuitous evil.

Keywords: evil, suffering, theism, theodicy, God

ISBNs: 9781108822879 (PB), 9781108906487 (OC)
ISSNs: 2631-3014 (online), 2631-3006 (print)

Contents

1 The Problem of Evil in Monotheism

All of us are familiar with evil in the world. Cancer and other diseases kill and debilitate thousands of people every year. Violence is common in political hotspots around the globe. Floods, hurricanes, and a myriad of other natural disasters destroy lives and communities. As sociologist Peter Berger states in *The Sacred Canopy*, every religion must make sense of evil by positing some higher meaning or authority – in effect, covering evil under a sacred canopy of explanation (1967: 53–4). In fact, perhaps more than anything else, the way a religion navigates the question of evil reveals how it understands the meaning of life. Prehistoric and primitive religions contain their own understandings, if only implicit, of why evil exists; developed religions with more sophisticated intellectual traditions address the problem of evil explicitly.

Among the religions of the world, monotheistic religion arguably faces the most difficult challenge from evil because monotheism makes (according to its own standards) the loftiest claims about the character and purposes of the divine: that a God who is omnipotent, omniscient, and perfectly good created the world. Each of the three great monotheistic religions – Judaism, Christianity, and Islam – faces both the generic problem of evil for monotheism and problems of evil specific to its more particular beliefs. Briefly reviewing the historical context out of which monotheistic belief arose provides perspective for understanding the significance of the problem of evil for these monotheisms.

Prehistoric and Polytheistic Religions

Evolutionary anthropologists have found that the emergence of religious instincts and behaviors followed closely upon the appearance of abstract, symbolic thought in *Homo sapiens*. Since we have no written history of early humanity, we are left with the task of reconstructing the cognitive world of early humans from both discovered artifacts and field observations of primitive tribes living today. For instance, an impressive degree of abstract and symbolic thought is demonstrated in the spectacular cave paintings in southwestern Europe dating from the Upper Paleolithic Period. Archaeological digs have also revealed burial practices that suggest some belief in life after death and signal the beginning of an early form of religion.

Animism as a tribal form of religion became an integral part of primitive human culture, probably aiding social cohesion and promoting group survival. Since preliterate and prescientific people lived close to nature, often encountering natural objects and natural forces that they did not fully understand, they explained many occurrences by ascribing a living soul or force (Latin: *anima*) to things in their environment, such as animals, plants, rivers, and mountains.

Furthermore, they believed in a mystical power or *mana* that permeates the world and thought that certain objects and persons have more *mana* than others – for example, a burial ground or the chieftain. Totems were often fashioned to resemble some animal whose power the tribe particularly admired so that they could share in its *mana*. For the primitive, the whole world was alive, and it was a wondrous yet dangerous place in which most religious behavior aimed at group cooperation and survival. Of course, the animist experienced pain, suffering, and death, but there was no assumption of a moral deity or moral universe, and there was no culture of intellectual reflection on such matters. Interaction with spiritual forces was largely for pragmatic and prudential reasons (Durkheim 1995).

During the Neolithic period, various national cultures began to conceptualize more specific spiritual beings or gods with a diversity of special powers and functions, such as care over life or the sea or death. National polytheisms, which were pervasive in the Ancient Near East, envisioned whole prehistories of the gods – that is, stories of how they came to be and how their existence supported the social order. Assyriologist Samuel Noah Kramer explains that the various polytheisms shared a common source in Sumerian religious thought (Kramer 1981). A Sumerian cuneiform clay tablet dating to the third millennium BC portrays an elaborate polytheistic perspective. Often referred to as "Eridu Genesis," this Sumerian writing portrays a primeval sea that engendered both heaven and earth and from whose union came the god of the air, Enlil, who in turn created humankind. Other gods also evolved in Sumerian thinking, each with a particular role – for instance, Enki created humans, Ereshkigal ruled the underworld, and Ninhursag oversaw the fertility of humans and the earth.

After Sumer, polytheistic thought patterns appear in all Ancient Near Eastern civilizations – Akkadia, Babylonia, and Egypt, and the like – with pantheons of multiple gods and their various functions. Not only did the gods require obeisance, so too did earthly kings or pharaohs who claimed to be their offspring. The Sumerians, for example, believed that their deities resided in heaven. They also believed that a statue of a god was a physical embodiment of that god, which in turn generated the need for priests and attendants who would give it care and attention, including leading official prayers, making sacrifices, and laying out special feasts. Thus, a deity's physical temple was that god's literal residence. Relating properly to these gods was considered vitally important to individual circumstances and societal welfare. Good and evil circumstances were ultimately interpreted through the template of polytheistic understanding as caused by angry or morally defective gods or the human failure to please these gods in some way.

Some scholars indicate that the unifying thread running through all polytheisms is "the mythic mode of thought" – which is a way of looking at the world that assumes ultimate continuity of the divine, the human, and the natural. Linkage between these three realms is evident in mythic narratives in which the gods come from some primeval natural state, often chaos, and then oversee various domains of nature. Ancient humans prayed, sacrificed, and engaged in religious rituals to influence the gods to be favorable to the circumstances of their lives. In response, the gods were thought to help or hurt humans by doing something in nature, such as granting victory or defeat in battle, blessing or ruining the harvest, and the like (Frankfort *et al.* 1977).

For the ancients who lived close to nature, it is not surprising that the theme of fertility pervaded their religious outlook. Femaleness was a key symbol of fertility, making the fertility-goddess important in all polytheistic religions. Scholars have designated this as the "Isis cult" in the ancient Mediterranean world – typified by Inanna for the Sumerians, Ishtar for the Assyrians, and Isis for the Egyptians (Calame 2008). Indeed, many of life's ultimate mysteries – regarding the origins of the world, humanity, or the gods themselves – were often explained by reference to some process akin to generative sexual activity. These mysteries display the inability of the ancient polytheisms, which were the most advanced religions in the world at the time, to conceptualize religious realities outside the framework of nature and its processes.

Since the mythic mode of thought was based on what we might call the continuity principle that assumes divine–nature–human interconnectedness, ancient polytheism was again largely prudential rather than moral because the gods were thought to be subject to human influence and manipulation. That is, humans could essentially do something within nature – bargains, magical incantations, sacrifices – to influence the gods. Of course, the gods were usually identified with various natural forces or objects, were anthropomorphized with human traits and even foibles, and were frequently arbitrary with humans, showing favor to some, disfavor to others, and indifference to most. Such were conceptual resources in the ancient world to explain the existence, aspirations, failures, and sufferings of humanity (Adogbo 2010). It was into this ancient polytheistic milieu that monotheism arose as its fierce, unrelenting opponent.

The Appearance of Hebrew Monotheism

Monotheism – the belief in one supreme God – entered the ancient world through the patriarch Abraham. The book of Genesis, which is the first book of the Hebrew Bible and the Christian Old Testament, records that Abraham, a nomadic leader in the early second millennium BC in Mesopotamia, was called by the one true God to journey to Canaan where he was to settle and have many progeny (Gen. 12:1–3). The covenant between God and Abraham was essentially that the Hebrew people would be given their own land of great blessing. As the narrative develops, the Hebrews experience good times and bad, famine and prosperity, times of trusting God and times of falling away, but they are led and protected by God as they, in effect, pursue nationhood.

The book of Exodus records that Moses took the Hebrew people further, rising up as the great prophet who led them out of slavery in Egypt and remained their leader for four decades, dying just before they entered Canaan, the land they believed God promised to them. After the Hebrews left Egypt, they journeyed in the wilderness close to Canaan, where Moses went to the top of Mt. Sinai and received the Ten Commandments from God, who appeared as "a bush that burns and is not consumed" (Exod. 3:2). The Ten Commandments were taken to reflect the intentions of the one true God who is holy, perfectly good, and therefore expects moral righteousness from his followers. Here is the root not simply of monotheism but of what is often called *ethical monotheism*.

Monotheistic scriptures may borrow some linguistic symbolism from surrounding polytheistic cultures, but their underlying theological message is monotheistic. Take the book of Genesis, for example. Strong monotheistic commitment is reflected in the early lines of the creation story in Genesis, which is traditionally attributed to Moses:

> In the beginning God created the heavens and the earth. The earth was without form, and void; and darkness was on the face of the deep. And the Spirit of God was hovering over the face of the waters. Then God said, "Let there be light"; and there was light. And God saw the light, that it was good; and God divided the light from the darkness. God called the light Day, and the darkness He called Night. So the evening and the morning were the first day.
>
> (Gen. 1:1–5)

The words "in the beginning God created" sweep away any notion of a prehistory to God because God is positioned as the single, sovereign, eternal, personal being who brings everything else into existence.

In Genesis, creation does not result from the sexual union between primeval gods, nor from a cosmic struggle, nor from some preexisting substance. Neither does primordial nature give rise to the gods; instead, nature is simply a creature, a contingent realm that is given finite existence by an infinite creator.

For the Hebrew mind, the absolute discontinuity between the transcendent God and nature, Creator and creature, directly countered the continuity principle that shaped polytheism. Thus, while the Genesis creation story uses literary imagery (the serpent, the forbidden fruit, etc.) that is quite familiar in the polytheistic ancient world, the conceptual themes of the Genesis creation story are distinctly monotheistic. Consider the sharp contrast with the *Enuma Elish*, the ancient Babylonian polytheistic writing in which Marduk, the god of order, kills the sea monster Tiamat, the symbol of primeval chaos. The monster's body becomes the earth and her blood becomes humanity – not an auspicious beginning to everything. Yet, in Genesis, God simply wills that the creation exists, and it comes into being; God pronounces it good, and its great value is established (Hasel 1974: 81–102).

In Christian history, the Fourth Lateran Council in 1215 AD carefully articulated the doctrine of creation as "creation out of nothing" (Latin *creatio ex nihilo*), thus emphasizing this important intellectual distinctive. Monotheism asserts that God alone exists from all eternity and created everything that is not himself; everything else is creature. Imagine the offense to Egyptian polytheism – in which the sun is a god, *Ra*, the highest deity in Egypt – that was caused by the Genesis statement that God brought the sun into being as a mere creature. Of course, this point was not lost on Moses, who was brought up and educated in the courts of Pharaoh.

Monotheism, then, is an entirely revolutionary idea inserted into the ancient world – denying divine–nature–human continuity and strongly asserting ontological discontinuity. Humans cannot trick or magically coerce this one God but must relate to God on moral grounds and live up to God's good purposes for them. This amazing idea overshadows polytheistic notions of petulant, self-concerned gods who often pursued less than noble purposes and were influenced by human deception or flattery. Interestingly, monotheism even gives foundation to an enlightened idea of history as linear, denying notions of fate or divine determinism and eliminating the cyclical idea of time. Thus, for monotheism, the world becomes the context for divine–human interaction, and history becomes the unfolding story of that interaction in which there is both progress and meaning.

Turning to the creation of humans specifically, we find this line in the first chapter of Genesis: "God created man in his own image, in the image of God he created him; male and female created he them" (Gen. 1:27). For the Judeo-Christian tradition, humans are unique creatures, with a special connection to God, because they are made "in the image of God." At a minimum, this idea has been understood to entail that humans, while physically embodied beings, have finite characteristics reflecting God's infinite characteristics, such as rationality, will, and the capacity for interpersonal relationships. We briefly note here that the monotheistic God is infinite personal spirit and that talk of the "image of God" is usually considered to be about the intangible traits of personhood in finite embodied persons. Furthermore, since the monotheistic God is nonphysical and nonbiological, and thus nonsexual, no human sex resembles God more than another, contrary to long-standing patriarchal misunderstandings; yet, for purposes of our discussions of God, traditional masculine pronouns are used herein without any ontological commitment that God is sexed or linguistic commitments that God is gendered.

Similarly, in Islam, a well-attested hadith declares that Allah created Adam "in his image" (Melchert 2011: 113–24), a teaching that accents the special status of humanity. Since Qur'an also clearly affirms the theme of divine transcendence, which denies that any created thing is "like" Allah (Qur'an 42:11), the status of humanity in Islam requires a bit more clarification. On this matter, Muslim thinkers explain that there cannot be any physical likeness of Allah but that human beings resemble Allah in having finite attributes that resemble Allah's attributes, such as knowledge and will, and particularly moral capacity (Ali Shah 2012: 6).

The profound cognitive content of monotheism is embraced by all three Abrahamic faiths as crucial to their orthodox viewpoints. William A. Irwin states, "Israel's great achievement, so apparent that mention of it is almost trite, was monotheism" (1977: 224). Monotheism thus marked a radical advance in the religious development of the human race and eventually generated further implications that had significant historical impacts – in offering important understandings of the nature of science, the nature of the human person, inherent and equal human rights, and the role of the political state (O'Connor and Oakley 1969). It is difficult to overestimate monotheism's positive influence over many centuries in these areas.

As we shall soon see, the problem of evil gets its particular potency because of the intellectual, moral, and spiritual exceptionalism of authentic monotheism. Some religion scholars dilute the utter uniqueness of Abrahamic monotheism by employing a broader concept of monotheism. For example, "The Great Hymn to Aten" from ancient Egypt has been cited as early evidence of monotheism. However, this document, which is attributed to Pharoah Akehnaten in the fourteenth century BC, actually reflects the attitude of henotheism – the worship of a single god while not denying the existence of other gods. The religion of Zoroastrianism, originating in Persia in the sixth century BC, is also incorrectly cited as a kind of monotheism. Zoroastrianism depicts the cosmos as involved in a great struggle between supremely Good and Evil forces. The good force, epitomized in Ahura Mazda, is the head of the universe, but the teachings about an uncreated destructive evil force, Angra Mainyu, essentially make Zoroastrianism a form of cosmic dualism.

Even Hinduism has been interpreted monotheistically, largely because of the ultimacy of Brahman, the Great Soul of the World, that is manifested in uncountably many gods such as Vishnu and Shiva. Although some religion scholars argue that the Vedic scriptures are monotheistic because they treat each deity, in turn, as supreme, this practice actually reflects the well-known attitude of kathenotheism, not that of ethical monotheism. Besides, in the Upanishads, Brahman is beyond all predication, which means that Brahman cannot be accurately termed powerful or good in ways that exclude the opposite qualities. Hinduism, then, is actually a form of pantheism (sometimes labeled "panentheism"), which is hardly a legitimate monotheism that confidently makes important assertions about God's nature, attributes, and purposes. Leaving further debates about proto-monotheisms and quasi-monotheisms for the interested reader to pursue in another venue, we turn now to the way the problem of evil arises for ethical monotheism.

Monotheism and Evil

Among all the religions – and types of religion – of the world, it seems that the monotheistic God is the deity whose creation would most certainly not include evil. After all, this transcendent deity is all-powerful and thus able to create whatever he wills. Indeed, this God is said to have created "out of nothing," without resistance from some primordial material or opposition from other gods. Furthermore, the monotheistic God is wholly good and wills the best for his creation, a stark contrast to the god of pantheism that includes both good and evil, as well as to polytheistic gods that feud among themselves or display petty jealousies toward humans. Finally, since the monotheistic God is all-knowing, God would know how to create the kind of world he wills in his perfect goodness.

While nonmonotheistic religions treat evil in other ways – the other side of the divine, outside total control of the divine, and the like – monotheism accents God's opposition to evil. This then makes the presence of evil in the world deeply problematic. The tension between these two monotheistic commitments can be readily seen:

    1. God is omnipotent, omniscient, and wholly good.

and

    2. Evil exists in God's created world.

Monotheism – or "theism" in its shortened form – must somehow eliminate the apparent incompatibility between these two assertions.

This study approaches the problem of evil as a philosophical problem dealing with the incompatibility – either logical or evidential – between these two propositions. However, in a larger sense, the problem of evil is not one problem but several problems, often intertwined, to be traced through the following sections. The well-known philosophical problem is discussed based on what can be known or rationally supported apart from sacred scripture or religious dogma. However, there are other dimensions of the problem of evil that require examination as well. The second problem that we will treat is the theological problem of evil, which includes additional ideas from a given theistic tradition in both forming and trying to answer the challenge of God and evil. Third, the religious problem of evil concerns why a person could or should have faith in God in light of his or her own experience of evil and suffering – in effect, exploring the question, why worship God? Fourth, the practical problem of evil focuses on the urgent need to work proactively against evil, often as the outgrowth of religious commitment. Fifth is the existential problem of evil, which pertains to how the individual makes meaning and value out of his or her life in the face of evil and suffering. Sixth, the pastoral problem of evil relates to how a religious believer might comfort or counsel others who experience evil and suffering. As our brief treatment of the problem of evil for monotheism unfolds, we engage these different dimensions, show how they intertwine, and assess the state of the discussion (for further study, see Peterson 2017).

2 The Problem in Culture and Philosophy

Suffering, disaster, injustice, and other forms of evil are ever present in our world, eliciting responses such as sympathy, compassion, anger, and even puzzlement. The depth of these subjective human responses leads some thinkers to underestimate the more reflective intellectual aspect of the problem. Religion scholar John Bowker writes that the problem of evil and suffering is not a rational difficulty so much as a deeply emotional one: "There is nothing theoretical or abstract about it. To talk of suffering is to talk not of an academic problem but of the sheer bloody agonies of existence, of which all men are aware and have direct experience" (1970: 2). Pragmatist philosopher William James states that the problem of evil is best treated as pertaining to our "inner attitude" – how we will face the world – and not to "systematic philosophy," which seeks to fit evil into an overall rational system (1961: 86). These thinkers properly identify other aspects of the problem (emotional, attitudinal, and the like). They do not take the problem of evil lightly, but they do fail to acknowledge the importance of the philosophical dimension of the problem, which is key to understanding. Indeed, not knowing how to make rational sense of evil is itself a form of suffering.

The Problem of Evil in Great Literature

Evil is a major theme in great literature, which is capable of portraying actual evil in gripping and concrete ways. Some literature even puts the philosophical problem in sharp focus. A prime example is found in Fyodor Dostoevsky's classic novel *Brothers Karamazov* (1976) in the poignant reunion of Ivan and Alyosha Karamazov, two brothers long separated by the odysseys of their different lives. Ivan is a university-educated atheist, and Alyosha is an apprentice monk in the Russian Orthodox church

Ivan challenges Alyosha's religious faith by telling stories of unthinkably inhumane evil:

> By the way, a Bulgarian I met lately in Moscow . . . told me about the crimes committed by the Turks and Circassians in all parts of Bulgaria through fear of a general rising of the Slavs. They burn villages, murder, rape women and children, they nail their prisoners to the fences by the ears, leave then till morning, and in the morning they hang them – all sorts of things you can't imagine. People talk sometimes of bestial cruelty, but that's a great injustice and insult to the beast; a beast can never be so cruel as a man, so artistically cruel. The tiger only tears and gnaws, that's all he can do. (1976: 219)

Ivan reveals that he collects such stories, particularly stories of cruelty to innocent children – the parents who locked their bed-wetting daughter in an outhouse on a cold Russian winter night, the landowner who set his hunting dogs on a stable boy, and more – and demands a rational answer from his devout brother.

Alyosha tries to assure him that everything works out for good in God's plan, resulting in a "higher harmony" that we cannot perceive. In opposition, Ivan insists that he cannot accept a system of religious belief that fails to make sense of the evils of life in terms of the categories of understanding we have:

> With my pitiful, earthly, Euclidean understanding, all I know is that there are none guilty; that cause follows effect, simply and directly; that everything flows and finds its level – but that's only Euclidean nonsense, I know that, and I can't consent to live by it! (1976: 224)

Ivan's response is that unless he can make sense of God's goodness intellectually, he must reject God in moral protest. In the towering figure of Ivan, his questions and demands, the intellectual problem is powerfully represented.

Great literature in Western culture grapples not only with humanly caused evils but also with evils of pain and suffering in nature. *The Plague* by Albert

Camus and *The Lisbon Earthquake* by Voltaire only begin the list of master-pieces in this regard (Larrimore 2000; Peterson 2017). William Blake's poem "The Tyger" rhythmically describes the lethal traits of this fearful beast as created by God and then asks the question, "Did he who made the Lamb make thee?" (1956: 1060–1). The poem recognizes God's power to frame the beast but raises the concern about whether God's putative goodness would "dare" to create it.

Literature can creatively explore the problem of evil as it is felt and perceived in broader culture, yet direct philosophical treatment of the problem sheds light on literary treatments and whatever practical, religious, and existential aspects of the problem emerge. Because the philosophical problem concerns the truth, credibility, and consistency of theism, no significant progress can be made without engaging the philosophical problem.

Definitions and Distinctions

Historically, the problem of evil has always received serious attention within the philosophy of religion, but the philosophical literature on God and evil has exploded since the 1970s. Much of this explosion is due to the general resurgence of philosophy of religion within analytic philosophy. Interestingly, the aims of analytic philosophy – such as conceptual clarity, terminological precision, and argumentative rigor – are now pursued in the problem of evil, taking the discussion in a technical direction. In Anglo-American philosophical circles, the debate over monotheism and evil has been engaged extensively by Christian philosophers and their nontheistic critics. The definitions and categories used to analyze the issues in this arena allow us to see the structure of the issues for Jewish and Islamic traditions as well.

In most discussions, the term *monotheism* (from Greek: *monos* meaning "one" and *theos* meaning "god") is shortened to *theism* (*theos*). Of course, theism is not itself a living religion but is the common conceptual core of the three living Abrahamic religions. William Rowe and other critics state that the debate is about *restricted standard theism*: the belief that there exists an omnipotent, omniscient, wholly good being who created the world. When any other beliefs are conjoined with restricted standard theism, some form of expanded standard theism is formed. Beliefs about Jesus as God incarnate, Allah's wise purposes, or YHWH's chosen people merely begin other beliefs that theists might want to include in the discussion. However, both theists and critics typically believe that if evil makes restricted standard theism rationally untenable, it makes all forms of expanded standard theism untenable.

The definition of the term *evil* also requires clarification since it has proven historically to be difficult to specify. Is it roughly equivalent to sin? Or is it more broadly all the negatives of life? Since the meaning of "evil" could be debated indefinitely, Edward Madden and Peter Hare recommend using "evil" to cover a range of commonly recognized evil without attempting a precise definition. Things that virtually everyone would call "evil" include, at the very least, extreme pain and suffering, the prosperity of bad people, the demise of good people, unfulfilled potential, damaged social relations, and numerous character defects, as well as physical disease, deformity, and dysfunction (Madden and Hare 1968: 6).

Although evil indeed has many faces with which we are all too familiar, one helpful classification distinguishes two basic types of evil – *moral evil* and *natural evil*. Moral evil is evil that results from human action; natural evil is evil that is due to the activity of nature. The two types of evil allow us to divide the general problem of evil into two subsidiary problems: the problem of moral evil and the problem of natural evil. Further subdivisions of problems of evil are also possible, such as the problem of animal pain. These categories will prove helpful as we proceed.

In philosophy, what is commonly called the problem of evil is actually an argument that employs the existence of evil (or some type of evil) against the existence of the theistic God. Of course, all arguments have a definite structure with premises supporting a conclusion. Thus, a "problem" presented by an argument from evil occurs when the premises of the argument are credible on some grounds to the theistic believer and yet its atheistic conclusion must be avoided. Since there are only two broad ways to rebut any argument – find fault with its logic or with one or more premises – theists pursue these two routes to reject some version of the argument while nontheistic critics defend the argument. An important distinction in the literature is between deductive arguments from evil and arguments that are construed inductively.

The Logical Argument from Evil

In 1955, J. L. Mackie carefully formulated the problem of evil as a deductive argument in a way that expressed what many professional philosophers had always thought. What is now called the logical argument from evil (also called the *a priori* problem and the deductive problem) is based on an alleged logical inconsistency between within theistic belief. As Mackie writes, "Here it can be shown, not that religious beliefs lack rational support, but that they are positively irrational, that several parts of the essential theological doctrine are inconsistent with one another" (1955: 200). Mackie states the inconsistency this way:

> God is omnipotent; God is wholly good; and yet evil exists. There seems to be some contradiction between these three propositions, so that if any two of them were true the third would be false. But at the same time all three are essential parts of most theological positions; the theologian, it seems, at once *must* adhere and *cannot consistently* adhere to all three. (1955: 200)

The apparently inconsistent triad – involving omnipotence, perfect goodness, and evil – resembles David Hume's formulation (following Epicurus):

> Is [God] willing to prevent evil, but not able? Then he is impotent. Is he able, but not willing? Then he is malevolent. Is he both able and willing? Whence then is evil? (1948: 66)

Critics insist that theists must reject at least one part of the triad, but theists offer responses to alleviate the logical pressure.

Some formulations of the logical inconsistency argument include reference to God's unlimited knowledge with maximal power and goodness in order, but let us continue here with Mackie's presentation:

(1) God is omnipotent;
(2) God is perfectly good;
(3) Evil exists.

Propositions (1) and (2) are standard theist claims, while proposition (3) is the theistic affirmation of evil in the world. In order to make the inconsistency explicit, Mackie offers definitions of key terms:

> [T]he contradiction does not arise immediately; to show it we need some additional premises, or perhaps some quasi-logical rules connecting the terms "good," "evil," and "omnipotent." The additional principles are that good is opposed to evil, in such a way that a good thing always eliminates evil as far as it can, and that there are no limits to what an omnipotent thing can do. From these it follows that a good omnipotent thing eliminates evil completely, and then the propositions that a good omnipotent thing exists, and that evil exists, are incompatible. (1955: 209)

Also, for the sake of completeness, Mackie assumes that evil is not logically necessary.

The Free Will Defense

Mackie's tightly reasoned case called forth a likewise precisely reasoned response from theistic philosopher Alvin Plantinga in 1967. Plantinga argued that the burden of proof falls upon the critic to prove inconsistency: "[T]o make good his claim the theologian must provide some proposition which is either necessarily true, or essential to theism, or a logical consequence of such propositions" (1955: 117). Clearly, there is no logical problem if the theist *qua* theist is not committed to each proposition in the set or if the set does not really entail a contradiction.

Let us merge (1) and (2) into the fuller theistic proposition:

(G) God is omnipotent, omniscient, and perfectly good.

Then let us relabel (3) as follows:

(E) Evil exists.

The charge of inconsistency is that it is logically impossible for (G) and (E) to be true together. Whereas *theodicy* is the traditional theistic enterprise of providing *plausible* reasons for God's permission of evil, Plantinga points out that here the theist needs only a *possible* reason to show consistency – that it is logically possible that both (G) and (E) be true. Offering a possible reason is what Plantinga calls a *defense*, an argument why the opponent's argument fails.

How would an argument for the consistency of (G) and (E) proceed? Plantinga follows the method for proving consistency between any two propositions *p* and *q* – which is to specify some proposition *r* that is consistent with *p* and, together with *p*, entails *q*. Now, the proposition *p and r* is possible, and thus describes a possible state of affairs, such that if *p and r* were true, *q* would also be true; hence, both *p* and *q* would be true. Consistency between *p* and *q* – the opposite of inconsistency – is thereby proved.

Plantinga argues for the consistency of (G) and (E) by seeking a third proposition in a story inspired by St. Augustine that pertains to God's reason for giving creatures free will. The Augustinian-type story goes as follows. A world containing creatures who are significantly free (and freely perform more good than evil actions) is more valuable, all else being equal, than a world containing no free creatures at all. God in his goodness chose to create human creatures and endow them with freedom to choose either good or evil. However, God cannot cause or determine free creatures to do only what is right because this would abrogate their freedom. Thus, in creating creatures capable of moral good, God thereby creates creatures capable of moral evil. As it turned out, some human creatures freely chose to go wrong, committing moral evil. Yet, the fact that free creatures sometimes go wrong counts neither against God's omnipotence nor against his goodness, for God could have prevented the occurrence of moral evil only by eliminating the possibility of moral good. As Plantinga puts it, the heart of the Free Will Defense is the following claim:

> [I]t is possible that God could not have created a universe containing moral good (or as much moral good as this world contains) without creating one that also contained moral evil. And if so, then it is possible that God has a good reason for creating a world containing evil. (2008: 347–9)

God's reason in this possible story, then, is his aim to achieve a valuable world, a very good world that contains the great gift of free will, which makes possible moral and spiritual life and the goods that come with it. Such a divine aim, Plantinga contends, exemplifies profound goodness. Since it is possible that God gave creatures significant free will, Mackie's definition of goodness is neither a necessary truth nor a theistic commitment. Thus, for Plantinga, goodness may not eliminate all evil within its power. Thus, there is no inconsistency between (G) and (E).

However, Mackie and other critics (see Flew 1955: 149) buttress the inconsistency charge by arguing that there are logically possible worlds containing free creatures and no evil. Mackie writes:

> God was not, then, faced with a choice between making innocent automata and making beings who, in acting freely, would sometimes times go wrong; there was open to him the obviously better possibility of making beings who would act freely but always go right. Clearly, his failure to avail himself of this possibility is inconsistent with his being both omnipotent and wholly good. (1955: 209)

This marks a crucial point of contention that allowed Plantinga to strengthen his argument even further.

Plantinga identified Mackie's position as *compatibilism* – the view that free will is compatible with being determined – while stating that the Free Will Defense assumes *incompatibilism* – the view that free will is incompatible with being determined. He labeled Mackie's compatibilist mistake "Leibniz's Lapse": the belief that it is a necessary truth that God, if omnipotent, could have actualized any possible world. A *possible world* is a *total way things could have been*, a *maximal state of affairs*. Although there are possible worlds containing moral good but no moral evil, the free will defender claims that the following is possible:

> God is omnipotent, and it was not within his power to bring about a world containing moral good but no moral evil.

Thus, an analysis of omnipotence requires more than recognizing that it is intrinsically possible that persons always do the right thing.

Fundamental to the free will defender's case is a certain understanding of the metaphysics of freedom in relation to omnipotence. Plantinga explains the concept of *being free with respect to an action*: If a person is free with respect to a given action x, then she is free to perform x or to refrain from performing x; no antecedent conditions and/or causal laws determine that she will perform the action or that she will not perform it. Thus, not even God can guarantee the outcome of free choice. It is apparent, then, that Mackie committed the Leibnizian mistake of failing to distinguish between states of affairs that are intrinsically possible in themselves and states of affairs that are intrinsically possible *for God* to bring about. For example, the state of affairs consisting in *Allyson freely repenting* is logically possible, but the state of affairs consisting in *God's bringing it about that Allyson freely repents* is not logically possible.

The effectiveness of the Free Will Defense was questioned in relation to other inconsistency problems related to God and evil. First, granting that God and evil are not inconsistent, perhaps the existence of God is inconsistent with the amount of evil this world contains. Surely, God could have created a world with less evil, perhaps by giving free creatures stronger desires to go right. Yet, although the world could contain less evil, the metaphysics of free will again entail that God cannot control the amount of evil that exists. As Plantinga argues, for any person P with significant free will, in whatever possible world where P is free with respect to a given action A, then it is *possible* that P go wrong with respect to A. Of course, it is also possible that P go right with respect to A, but the choice is up to P. The free will defender's point, then, is that *possibly* it was not within God's power to create a world containing as much moral good but less moral evil than the actual world contains. Once again, the charge of inconsistency is defeated.

Second, granting that the Free Will Defense handles questions about God and moral evil, perhaps the existence of God is incompatible with natural evil. After all, natural objects and processes do not have free will such that God cannot prevent them from causing harm. Plantinga offers two lines of response to this problem. One point he makes is that it is possible that some evils are connected to great goods:

> [It] is conceivable that some natural evils and some persons are so related that the persons would have produced less moral good if the evils had been absent. Some people deal creatively with certain kinds of hardship or suffering, acting in such a way that on balance the whole state of affairs is valuable. And perhaps the response would have been less impressive and the total situation less valuable if the evil had not taken place. (2008: loc. 669)

Various moral virtues such as courage, compassion, and perseverance are not possible without danger, hardship, and other difficult situations. So natural evil is possible in a theistic universe.

Another point Plantinga makes is that natural evil may also be a form of moral evil. It is *possible*, he argues, that natural evil is caused by the free actions of nonhuman spirits: Satan and his minions. Augustine believed that this was actually *true*, but the free will defender need only claim that it is *logically possible* and compatible with (G). The Free Will Defense, then, turns on the following claim: *possibly* it was not within God's power to create a world containing a more favorable balance of good over evil with respect to the actions of the nonhuman persons it contains. Critics and some theists took Plantinga to be asserting the factual existence of malignant nonhuman spirits. However, he was simply extending the salient logical point of the Free Will Defense to refute the charge that there is an inconsistency between God and natural evil.

During the 1970s, philosophers increasingly acknowledged the strength of the Free Will Defense against the claim that evil is inconsistent with the existence of God. In place of the logical challenge, the objection emerged that the existence of evil (or perhaps the amount of it) somehow makes it *improbable* or *unlikely* that God exists, evolving into what is now called the evidential argument from evil (Plantinga 2008: loc. 690). This provides the focus of the next section.

3 The Problem of Gratuitous Evil

As the Free Will Defense was increasingly seen as an effective rebuttal of the logical argument, some critics developed an argument from evil that purported not that theism is internally inconsistent but that it is unlikely given the facts of evil. As this argument evolved, various formulations of it were labeled probabilistic, inductive, or *a posteriori* arguments from evil before the nomenclature "evidential argument from evil" became standard. Discussing the critical exchanges that ensued over this argument helps us gauge its strengths and weaknesses as well as the prospects for different avenues of response.

The Evolution of the Evidential Argument

Nontheists as well as most theists have shared the deep intuition that evil constitutes a serious problem for theistic belief, and the evidential argument emerged as a more promising formulation of the problem. Instead of charging that God and evil are logically incompatible, this new form of argument charged that God and evil are *probabilistically* incompatible: that the existence of evil makes the existence of God unlikely. For example, J. W. Cornman and Keith Lehrer argue that an all-good, all-knowing, and all-powerful God would not create a world like ours with so much suffering and evil:

> Given this world, then, . . . we should conclude that it is *improbable* that it was
> created or sustained by anything we would call God. Thus, given this
> particular world, it seems that we should conclude that it is improbable that
> God – who, if he exists, created the world – exists. Consequently, the belief
> that God does not exist, rather than the belief that he exists, would seem to be
> justified by the evidence we find in this world. (1970: 340–1)

Here we find a basic argument couched in the language of probability rather
than inconsistency.

Wesley Salmon offered a more technical probabilistic argument using the
evidence of evil against the theistic design argument in order to conclude that
the probability that this world was designed by an all-knowing, all-powerful,
and all-good being is low. Salmon invoked the frequency or statistical theory of
probability in reasoning that there are far more possible universes with this
much evil that are not divinely created than those that are divinely created
(1978: 143–76). The appearance of various probabilistic arguments from evil
elicited a comprehensive response from Alvin Plantinga, who argued that no
extant theory of probability – *statistical,* or *personalist,* or *logical* – is a viable
basis for an argument from evil (1979).

Among the obstacles for such arguments are the inherent troubles in modern
probability studies generally – for example, the lack of any clear criterion for
judging the probability of one statement on the basis of another and the function of
implicit background beliefs in assessing probability. Plantinga argued that it is
difficult to specify the exact relationship that supposedly holds between (E) and
(G) such that the former could be evidence against the latter and of calculating
without begging the question the degree to which (~G), which is the denial of (G),
is somehow more probable with respect to (E). Indeed, the recognition that
probability assessments are notoriously relative to one's *background assumptions*
or *total belief set* greatly damages the prospects for a viable frequency argument
from evil and becomes a controversial aspect of other probabilistic arguments
from evil as well. In the present context, this means that there is no reason to accept
the critic's assessment – based on her own background beliefs – that the antecedent
probability is low that God would create a world with the evil this one contains.

Nevertheless, most theistic and nontheistic thinkers continued to believe that
evil could be employed in some kind of broadly inductive (nondemonstrative)
argument against theism. The ground was being prepared for what would
become the most widely discussed version of the argument from evil.

The Evidential Argument from Evil

A viable formulation of an inductive argument from evil that would become the
main platform for discussion was going to depend not only on a new argument

strategy but also on a new statement of the evidence of evil and the case for it. In the early literature, three formulations of the evidence of evil were explored:

(E1) Evil exists;
(E2) Large amounts, extreme kinds, and perplexing distributions of evil exist;
(E3) Gratuitous evil exists.

Each statement of the evidence generates a distinct formulation of the evidential argument:

Versions of Evidential Argument from Evil

I	II	III
(E1)	(E2)	(E3)
is evidence	is evidence	is evidence
against	against	against
(G)	(G)	(G)

Although (E1) was central in the logical argument, most thinkers recognized that a stronger argument would be based on a stronger statement of the evidence because some evils obviously serve good purposes.

Walter Kaufmann used the stronger statement (E2), which creates Version II:

> The problem arises when monotheism is enriched with – or impoverished by – two assumptions: that God is omnipotent and that God is just. In fact, popular theism goes beyond merely asserting that God is just and claims that God is "good," that he is morally perfect, that he hates suffering, that he loves man, and that he is infinitely merciful, far transcending all human mercy, love, and perfection. Once these assumptions are granted, the problem arises: why, then, is there *all* the suffering we know? And as long as these assumptions are granted, this question cannot be answered. For if these assumptions were true, it would follow that there could not be all this suffering. Conversely: since it is a fact that there is *all this* suffering, it is plain that at least one of these assumptions must be false. Popular theism is refuted by the existence of *so much* suffering. The theism preached from thousands of pulpits and credited by millions of believers is disproved by Auschwitz and *a billion* lesser evils. (1961: 139; emphasis added)

Effectively accepting (E2), theologian Gordon Kaufman remarked that "[e]xploration of the *varieties*, *subtleties*, and *enormities* of evil in human life has become perhaps the principal theme of literature, art, and drama since World War II" (1973: 171–2; emphasis added). In more recent discussions, this point is made by speaking of the large amounts, extreme kinds, and perplexing distributions of evil. Potential theistic responses include claiming that there is no clear limit to the evils God might allow and that even severe evils might serve good purposes.

In 1979, William Rowe advanced an argument based on (E3), which is the strongest statement of the evidence, giving us Version III in the chart. Since some evils seems subject to reasonable explanation, the most serious *prima facie* evidence is constituted by evils for which no reasons seem available that would justify God in allowing them. Rowe's formulation of the argument became the progenitor of decades of discussion and debate:

(R1) There exist instances of intense suffering which an omnipotent, omniscient being could have prevented without thereby losing some greater good or permitting some evil equally bad or worse.

[Factual Premise]

(R2) An omniscient, wholly good being would prevent the occurrence of any intense suffering it could, unless it could not do so without thereby losing some greater good or permitting some evil equally bad or worse.

[Theological Premise]

Therefore,

(R3) There does not exist an omnipotent, omniscient, wholly good being.

[Atheistic Conclusion]

Since the logic of the argument is correct, discussion naturally turns to the premises, which are labeled above to denote their role in the argument (Rowe 1979: 336).

The Theological Premise contains a necessary but not a sufficient condition for an omnipotent, omniscient, wholly good being to permit suffering that he has the power to prevent:

(i) there is some greater good that God can obtain only if he permits the intense evil in question, *or*
(ii) there is some greater good that God can obtain only if he permits the intense evil or some other equally bad or worse evil, *or*
(iii) God can prevent the evil only if he permits some other evil equally bad or worse.

Thus, an evil is *gratuitous* (pointless, meaningless, unjustified) if it does not meet this three-part condition, which Rowe believes accords with our basic moral understanding. For present purposes, we shall simply say, an evil is gratuitous if it is not necessary to a greater good or to the prevention of an evil equally bad or worse. In effect, the argument involves the principle that *God would prevent or eliminate any gratuitous or pointless evil.*

Since most theists and nontheists agree that the Theological Premise (R2), is true, probable, or credible, it becomes the focus of debate – as theists attack it and nontheists support it. Rowe explains his rational support for (R1), which he says is rooted in the intense suffering, both animal and human, occurring daily in our world. Rowe's original formulation of the argument employed a representative case of gratuitous natural evil: a fawn dying horribly in a forest fire. Rowe argues that it is more reasonable than not to believe that this is an "apparently pointless" evil because it does not seem that there is any greater good for which it is necessary. Hence, there is inductive support for thinking that God has no *morally sufficient reason* for permitting such evils.

Rowe added moral evil to the evidence by including Bruce Russell's case of moral evil: a little girl beaten, raped, and murdered in Detroit (1989; see also Russell 1989). Addressing what became known as the cases of Bambi and Sue, Rowe continued to maintain his point about apparent gratuity. In interaction with critics, Rowe acknowledged that it is possible to be mistaken about one individual case of alleged gratuity but argued that it is not reasonable to believe that *all* instances of seemingly pointless animal and human suffering are non-gratuitous. Although Rowe revised his argument several times, the underlying structure did not change. His central claim remained clear: "[W]hen we consider horrendous evils or the sheer magnitude of human and animal suffering, the idea that an omnipotent, omniscient, perfectly good being is in control of the world may strike us as absolutely astonishing, something almost beyond belief" (1998: 533–4).

To aid our conceptualization, a trimmer version of the argument from gratuitous evil goes as follows:

(R1′) Gratuitous evils exist.
(R2′) If an omnipotent, omniscience, wholly good God exists, then gratuitous evils would not exist.

Therefore,

(R3′) God does not exist.

The argument structure is deductive, but the support for premise (R1′) – just as for Rowe's (R1) – is inductive, making the argument broadly inductive and appropriate to couch in the language of probability.

The Skeptical Theist Defense

Theists generally attempted to rebut Rowe's argument by attacking (R1) based on one of two strategies: either arguing that there are reasons to think it is false or arguing that there is no reason to think it is true. Traditional theodicies follow the first strategy, while what became known as the Skeptical Theist Defense follows the second strategy. This defense made a case for skepticism about belief in the factual claim (R1). Skeptical defense questioned the epistemic grounds for the factual claim that there is (or probably is) gratuitous evil. Stephen Wykstra argued that our finite intellectual capacities give us no reason to believe that we could discern all the connections between evils and known goods or know all the goods for the sake of which God allows evil. As Wykstra claimed, God's infinite knowledge vastly transcends our knowledge such that we do not have "reasonable epistemic access" to God's perspective on evils (1984: 85).

Wkystra specifically focuses on the epistemic use of Rowe's term "appears" – which pertains to what we are inclined to believe when we contemplate a given situation (1984: 80–1). According to Wykstra, Rowe's inductive support for (R1) moves from the proposition

(R4) It appears that some evils are connected to no outweighing goods

to the proposition

(R5) It is reasonable to believe that some evils are not connected to outweighing goods.

This reasoning has the general form: (A) It appears that p; therefore, (B) It is reasonable to believe that p. Such an inference is clearly consonant with various principles in mainline epistemology that affirm trusting our generally reliable belief-forming powers such as perception, memory, and the like (e.g., see Swinburne 2004: 246).

However, argues Wykstra, the Principle of Credulity fails in this context because it posits an epistemic relation between (A) and (B) above that does not meet his proposed Condition of Reasonable Epistemic Access (CORNEA):

> On the basis of cognized situation s, human H is entitled to claim "It appears that p" only if it is reasonable for H to believe that, given her cognitive faculties and the use she has made of them, if p were not the case, s would likely be different than it is in some way discernible by her.
> (1984: 85)

Rowe's appearance-claim assumes that, if there were God-justifying reasons for all sufferings, then it is likely that we would not have the blindness to them that we have. However, for Wykstra, it is not reasonable to believe this because an infinitely wise deity would surely know of outweighing goods that evade our finite understanding; we humans cannot reasonably expect to know all the goods in virtue of which God permits suffering.

Rowe counters that his argument targets *restricted standard theism* – which is the theistic position that there is an omnipotent, omniscient, wholly good being who created the world – whereas Wykstra invokes a form of expanded standard theism, which is restricted standard theism conjoined with one or more other propositions. Wystra's skeptical claim that humans cannot discern the goods for the sake of which God allows evil is simply not part of standard theism per se. Some versions of expanded theism are more affirming of the ability of human reason in these matters, a point we will pursue later.

Some other theistic thinkers also question whether there are sufficient epistemic grounds to affirm (R1). Michael Bergmann, for example, supports Skeptical Theism by arguing that it is quite likely that reality far outstrips our comprehension of it in many areas of life, making it unreasonable to think that we humans have reliable comprehension of the connections of goods and evils (2001). One response from Rowe employs what he calls the "good parent analogy" – observing that, even when a good parent allows a child to suffer pain for some good reason (such as a dental procedure) that the child does not understand, the parent is there to comfort and assure the child of his or her presence and abiding love. For Rowe, then, even granting a wide gap between divine and human comprehension, it is unbelievable that, during intense human suffering, a perfectly good being of infinite wisdom and power and love would seem distant, silent, and even absent. This point, Rowe argues, is completely independent of the previous point about whether the goods we know are representative of the goods there are (2001: 297–303). The interested reader is encouraged to study the further evolution of the debate between Rowe and Skeptical Theists, including the use of Bayesian probability calculations to determine the probability of the disputants' claims given prescribed background information (Dougherty and McBrayer 2014).

The Epistemic Status of the Factual Premise

The debate over whether it is rational to believe the factual premise may seem to be ultimately inconclusive, something like a rational stalemate. However, critics can insist that a stalemate works to the advantage of the nontheistic view because the theist has failed her responsibility to make sense of theistic claims about God's goodness and power. By contrast, many theists claim that there are other arguments that make the existence of God likely, but critics often counter that the traditional theistic arguments are unconvincing. All of this makes for a robust debate about the effectiveness of theistic arguments independent of their relation to the problem of evil (see Peterson *et al.* 2013: chap. 5). Furthermore, Alvin Plantinga maintains that belief in God can be rational without argumentative support and in spite of ostensible negative evidence – that is, that belief in God can be *properly basic*, which means that defense against the problem of evil would be sufficient to maintain rational belief in God (2000).

The position that belief in God can be properly basic under appropriate conditions has been called Reformed Epistemology. This position holds that human beings have various innate cognitive faculties (e.g., perception, memory, and even a sense of the divine) that can directly (immediately, noninferentially) produce warranted rational beliefs. Although Reformed Epistemology has generated much technical discussion within the Christian analytic philosophy of religion, it is only one of many discussions in monotheistic traditions regarding ways to think about the rationality of religious belief. But it is worth observing that, when considering the rationality of belief in God in light of evil, it is ideal to seek an all-things-considered evaluation – something like an assessment of theism on the *total evidence*, as it were – but we postpone further commentary on this until Section 4.

Short of a total evaluation of theism, what can be said here about the rational status of the factual claim that there is gratuitous evil? One important but seldom-taken theistic line of response is to agree with Rowe that it is more rational than not to believe there is gratuitous evil. To deem an evil gratuitous is to make a moral evaluation that is widely shared in the human community, despite the fact that we have an admittedly modest grasp of some very great goods (such as beatitude in God's presence) and perhaps do not have any grasp of other great goods. Nevertheless, the goods in dispute are largely those goods pertaining to our common human nature, which are reflected even in our dim imaginations of fulfillment in God's presence. Our essential humanity, then, accessed through both introspection and the common wisdom of the human race, grounds a generally reliable and widely agreed upon understanding of the types of goods and evils and their possible interrelations that are relevant to the kind of beings we are. Hence, it is staggering to think that we are hopelessly in the dark about such matters. So while it is logically possible that there are goods relevant to human nature that are beyond comprehension, and while it is surely highly probable that reality is far larger than our grasp of it, such considerations, in the final analysis, do not show that it is not reasonable to believe that there are gratuitous evils.

While the Skeptical Theist Defense, which is based on human epistemic limitations, may not be a successful undercutting defeater of the belief that that there is gratuitous evil, the history of monotheism contains another undercutting argument against belief in gratuitous evil that is worth briefly exploring. Within monotheism, Divine Command Theory – or what is commonly called *theological voluntarism* – can also be advanced to undercut the claim that there are states of affairs in this world that God, if God exists, is morally obligated not to permit. The theological voluntarist replies that there is no independent and objective moral standard for evaluating God because God's commanding (or willing) determines what is good. Unfortunately such a move disconnects human moral standards from God's morality and thus obviates the argument from evil, which at one level rests on a moral judgment.

We can readily detect among monotheistic religions a strong tradition of Natural Law Theory as a major alternative to Divine Command Theory, an alternative that has historically been the majority opinion regarding both morality and jurisprudence. Natural Law Theory claims that there are objective moral truths about how human beings should act and be treated – truths that pertain to our divinely created human nature and are known by divinely given moral capacities. This basic position, which is represented in many mainline versions of monotheism, emphasizes not God's will but God's wisdom. What Aquinas calls God's "right reason" (*recta ratio*) perfectly perceives what is objectively and intrinsically good.

Interestingly, this kind of theistic natural law thinking makes a ready case for the reasonableness of accepting the Factual Premise that there is gratuitous evil. Reasonable judgments that some evils are gratuitous – that is, unnecessary to any greater good – are tantamount to claiming that the world as a whole would have been better had those evils not occurred. In fact, such judgments fuel human moral actions to eliminate or alleviate many evils – actions that are encouraged by monotheistic preaching and teaching. It would, therefore, be very damaging for standard theism not to affirm the general reliability of our moral sense and the actions flowing from it. None of this is to suggest that theism entails that all judgments about gratuitous evils are invariably correct since some evils that initially appear gratuitous may be found upon investigation to be plausibly necessary to a greater good. However, it is to suggest that protecting theism by implicitly or explicitly holding that human moral experience is completely incompetent to appraise the gratuity of evils is, in the end, almost certainly an untenable approach.

In effect, then, moral realism – ontologically, about the moral standards involved, and epistemologically, about the moral capacities employed – supports the reasonableness of a Rowe-type judgment that there is gratuitous evil. Philosophically, moral realists – including theistic moral realists – argue that we must exercise a fundamental trust in our intellectual and moral faculties such that there is a presumption in favor of our considered judgments about gratuity.

Hence, on purely philosophical grounds, all other things held equal, we should be wary about dismissing or discrediting the more obvious by the less obvious.

There are also theological grounds for moral realism because, in their own ways, the monotheistic religions teach that human intellectual and moral capacities were created by God and somehow reflect God. Theology, as the study of God, is itself an achievement of these capacities – replete with claims about God's nature, goodness, and purposes. In orthodox Christianity, for example, there are far-reaching knowledge claims regarding God's Trinitarian nature and God's incarnation in Jesus Christ. Given the basic reliability of divinely created human powers for forming reasonable beliefs about such matters (often in interaction with scriptures, tradition, and the historical experience of the believing community), it is odd then to contend that there is no way to form reasonable beliefs about the gratuity of evils. Indeed, if we are systematically mistaken in judging the gratuity of various evils, that fact itself would be a strong candidate for a gratuitous evil. In the end, the price of both intellectual and moral skepticism about our evaluations of evil in the world is a price too high for a standard theist to pay.

Returning to our earlier question concerning the rational status of the factual claim that there is gratuitous evil, considerations for its credibility seem to outweigh those against its credibility. However, as long as some theists understand their theological position to entail the Theological Premise – that God cannot allow gratuity – they will always feel a need to find some way to discredit the Factual Premise, even at the price of putting theism in tension with the ordinary human experience of evil in the world as well as with some forms of expanded theism. Although the discussion thus far has engaged defensive attempts by theists to undercut the Factual Premise, theistic traditions also contain theodicies aimed at rebutting the Factual Premise by providing explanations of why evils are necessary to certain greater goods. It is to this enterprise of theodicy that we now turn in Section 4.

4 A Range of Theodicies

For monotheistic religions historically, theodicy rather than defense has been the predominant approach to the problem of evil. Theodicy reflects the intellectual obligation of a monotheistic position to provide a substantive explanation for evil in the world. The term "theodicy" itself derives from the Greek words *theos* (god) and *dikē* (justice) such that the enterprise of theodicy is understood as an attempt to justify the ways of God in light of evil. In this section, we discuss the nature of theodicy and examine several important theodicies available in monotheism, particularly those theodicies that have been robustly discussed by analytic Christian philosophers. In the next section, we broaden our consider of theodicies to explore commonalities and differences across theodicies in Christianity, Judaism, and Islam.

The Greater-Good Framework

Meta-theodicy – the consideration of the role and scope of theodicy – has been conceived of differently by different thinkers. For one thing, there is disagreement over the kinds of reasons for evil that theodicy needs. Some thinkers hold that theodicy must provide God's *possible* reasons for allowing evil while others believe that it must supply *plausible* reasons while a very few others think that it must provide God's *actual* reasons. For another thing, thinkers disagree over the scope of theodicy: should it attempt to explain a specific evil (e.g., Rowe's dying fawn) or more generally a class of evil (e.g., natural evil) or simply all evils? Amid these disagreements, there is widespread agreement that the explanatory work of a theodicy must account for what sorts of greater goods could not have been attained without the evils in question.

Contemporary philosophy of religion contains a great many "greater-good theodicies" that seek to counter Rowe-type evidential arguments. The core argument from Section 3 goes as follows:

(R1′) Gratuitous evils exist.

(R2′) If an omnipotent, omniscience, wholly good God exists, then gratuitous evils would not exist.

Therefore,

(R3′) God does not exist.

In Section 3, we saw that one or both premises of the argument must be refuted in order to avoid the atheistic conclusion. Rowe's own statement of Premise 1 asserts, "There exist instances of intense suffering which an omnipotent, omniscient being could have prevented without thereby losing some greater good or permitting some evil equally bad or worse" (1979: 337). In regard to difficult cases of suffering, Rowe typically claims that there does not appear to be any greater good such that the prevention of this case of suffering would require either the loss of a stated good or the occurrence of an evil equally bad or worse (Rowe 1979: 338). Since most theists accept the theological construal of Premise 2, skeptical theists and theodicists alike attack Premise 1. Skeptical theists seek to undercut it while theodicists seek to rebut it to stop the argument from going through. Theodicists have employed various themes positing greater goods that could not be obtained without the evils. Although a close, analytical theistic evaluation of Premise 2 can also be insightful – a point that we will pursue later in this section – we must first discuss some major greater-good theodicies.

The long history of greater-good theodicy in Western philosophy contains many themes, some major and recurring, others more minor and idiosyncratic. Among familiar themes for explaining evil are the following: evil provides a necessary contrast to the good; evil and suffering test moral and spiritual dedication; evil and suffering build character; evil and suffering will be compensated in the afterlife. Minor themes include the idea that evil and suffering are punishment for sin and that evil and suffering are caused by demonic forces. Yet, by far, the most well-known and influential themes are that moral evil is due to free will, that natural evil results from the operation of natural laws, and that a world containing suffering (as well as obvious goods) presents opportunities for spiritual growth and improvement. In all monotheisms, the greater-good explanatory framework is, so to speak, the "parent," and the various particular theodicies are its "offspring" (Stewart 1993).

Augustinian Theodicy

The dominant tradition in Christian theodicy in the Western World emanates from Augustine, a philosopher and theologian in the fourth century AD. In part, Augustine was rebutting Manichaeanism, a form of cosmic dualism that projected a cosmology of two equal but opposite cosmic powers, one good and the other evil, at war in the cosmos. The good power, which people worship, is identified with a spiritual world of light and order, but it is not singularly absolute or sovereign. The evil power, identified with darkness, also exerts influence, accounting for the strange mix of good and evil in the world. For Augustine, however, the Christian worldview entails that God is the unrivaled sovereign creator of all things and that no evil comes from him. So Augustine's theodicy tries to show how evil in the world in no way detracts from God's total sovereignty.

Augustine's vision of reality involves several strands of thought relevant to theodicy. One strand is the idea that God is supreme in both reality and goodness. Consequently, the universe – God's creation – is also good. Since only God has the power to bestow being, all creatures are good in their essence. In fact, Augustine reflects a traditional theme in Western philosophy: the linkage of being and goodness. Now, "being" here is not bare "existence" (which does not admit of degrees) but instead can have more or less "intensity" or greater or lesser degrees of reality. Intensity or reality, then, admits of degrees. In Augustine's terminology, everything has "measure, form, and order" (1953a: vi), which is its degree of being. God's rich and variegated

creation is thereby filled with all levels of being, and the goodness of all things is
correlated to the measure, form, and order God has given them. Thus, on the
scale of created things, an artichoke is more valuable than a rock, an antelope
more valuable than an artichoke, and a human being more valuable than an
antelope.

From Augustine's perspective, evil is not a being, not a thing. While evil can
be profoundly experienced by humans, evil does not, metaphysically speaking,
exist in its own right; it is not one of the substantial constituents of the universe.
Rather, evil is "privation," the lack of reality and thus the lack of goodness –
privatio boni (Augustine 1977: 174). This theme put in motion the idea in
Western Christianity that evil is defect, damage, degradation – a warping of
something fundamentally good. Put another way, evil is parasitic on created
reality, making it cease to function according to its given nature.

For Augustine, evil enters creation through the misuse of finite free will –
which theologically is "sin." Both natural and moral evils, he asserts, result
from the wrong choices of free rational beings. To explain how free rational
creatures – which represent a very valuable kind of being capable of mirroring
God in certain respects – can fall away from God, Augustine appeals to the
Christian doctrine of "creation out of nothing" (*creatio ex nihilo*). For him, since
creatures are brought into being "out of nothing," they are imperfect and
dependent, and are "mutable" or changeable, and thus, have the capability of
sin.

Augustine never quite resolved the unavoidable dilemma of accounting for
how an originally and unqualifiedly good creature could commit sin. On the one
hand, if the creature is perfect relative to its place in the scale of being, then it is
difficult to envision how it would ever commit sin. On the other hand, if the
creature is initially flawed and thus commits sin, it is difficult to see how to
exonerate God of blame. The dilemma pertains to angelic creatures as well, as
Schleiermacher noted: "the more perfect . . . good angels are supposed to have
been, the less possible it is to find any motive but those presupposing a fall
already, for example, arrogance and envy" (1928: 161). Unable to solve the
puzzle completely, Augustine could probe no further and simply appealed to
the divinely bestowed power of creaturely freedom (Augustine 1872: chaps.
9–11).

Of course, omniscience is classically taken to entail that God knew that creatures
would sin, but this makes God bear ultimate responsibility for a creation that would
fall. Augustine's view of God's predestination applies here. In Adam, the whole
human race sinned because the fall was "seminally present" in his loins (Augustine
1950: xiii, 14). Thus, humankind is guilty of sin and subject to condemnation.
However, in God's sovereignty, some persons are justly "predestined to

punishment" while others are mercifully "predestined to grace" (Augustine 1887: 100). In this fashion, Augustine subsumes the puzzles of free will under the mystery of sovereignty. Beyond this treatment of Augustine on evil, the interested student may want to pursue further some of the finer points – such as whether foreknowledge and predestination allow for robust human freedom.

Perhaps the finishing touch to Augustinian theodicy is its aesthetic picture of the universe under a sovereign God. For Augustine, the whole universe – fallen but being redeemed – is "beautiful" and "fitting" when seen from God's perspective. The different grades or kinds of creatures are somehow complementary in an overall scheme that is harmonious and balanced in the sight of God. The characteristics of each kind of creature, then, are appropriate to its place in the great hierarchy of created reality.

It may seem that the aesthetic theme explains natural evil better than it does moral evil, but Augustine applies it to moral evil by reference to justly deserved, properly proportioned punishment that settles accounts for wrongs committed. Augustine sees even the fall of the human race and the damnation of sinners as falling under the "perfection" and "beauty" of the universe (1953b: III. ix 26). He states, "For as the beauty of a picture is increased by well-managed shadows, so, to the eye that has skill to discern it, the universe is beautified even by sinners, though, considered by themselves, their deformity is a sad blemish" (1950: xi. 23). Everything, then, including natural and moral evils, contribute to the aesthetic beauty of the whole: "If it were not good that evil things exist, they would certainly not be allowed to exist by the Omnipotent Good" (Augustine 1948: xxiv. 96).

Clearly, Augustinian theodicy entails the denial of the factual premise of the argument from gratuitous evil because evil in the universe serves the higher harmony of God's sovereign design. Thus, there is no gratuitous evil, no state of affairs without which the universe would have been better. As Augustine says, "God judged it better to bring good out of evil than not to permit any evil to exist" (1948: viii. 27).

Irenaean Theodicy

A different orientation in theodicy, which comes from Irenaeus, a Bishop in the Eastern Church in the second century, was introduced into twentieth-century philosophy by John Hick, who articulated what he called "soul-making" theodicy using Irenaean themes. In his book *Evil and the God of Love*, Hick observes that while both Augustinian and Irenaean theodicy share the fundamental aim of absolving God of responsibility for evil, Augustinian thought looks back to the human fall historically whereas Irenaean thought looks forward to the future development of humanity in the divine plan.

According to Hick, Adam, the first human (along with the rest of the original creation) was created innocent and immature, with the privilege of becoming good by loving God and fellow creatures. The Augustinian error, according to Hick, equates original goodness with original perfection. However, Hick points out that, logically, God cannot create morally mature persons by fiat because moral maturity or anything approaching moral perfection entails struggling with temptation over time and perhaps even experiencing evil (1978: 255). Hence, Hick's Irenaean approach explains that evil is not a decline from pristine purity and goodness but is rather an inevitable stage in the gradual growth of the human race:

> I suggest ... that it is an ethically reasonable judgment, even though in the nature of the case not one that is capable of demonstrative proof, that human goodness slowly built up through personal histories of moral effort has a value in the eyes of the Creator which justifies even the long travail of the soul-making process. (1978: 256)

From this perspective, humanity was not created perfect but is, rather, in the process of being perfected. In this process, sin occurs when imperfect but developing creatures almost inevitably organize their lives apart from God.

For Irenaean theodicy, God's grand scheme is to help bring about the spiritual and moral maturity of immature human beings by placing them in an environment conducive to this goal. The environment must be one in which there are real challenges, real opportunities for the display of moral virtue, and real possibilities for expressing faith in God. This environment must involve a community of moral agents interacting in a variety of special ways – deciding on the kinds of relationships they will have, what projects they will pursue, and how they will live together. The soul-making environment must also include a physical order of impersonal objects operating independently of our wills: atoms and molecules, fields of energy, ocean currents, biological cells, and innumerable other material things. Obviously, this kind of environment presents opportunities for developing moral and spiritual qualities as well experiencing dangers like pain, failure, and ruin.

Interestingly, Hick deems it important to spiritual growth that the world appear "as if" there is no God – and evil plays an important role in this appearance. The religiously ambiguous appearance of the world – our inability to discern for sure if there is or is not a God – creates "epistemic distance" between creature and Creator, allowing the genuine exercise of faith (1978: 281). Hick argues that if the presence of God were borne in too strongly upon creaturely consciousness, it would actually eliminate the possibility of faith. Of course, God's hiddenness can have the opposite effect of making it virtually inevitable that many persons will not believe in God and will default to self-centered competition with other persons – which is a condition that Hick calls sin.

In regard to moral evil, Hick says that the possibility of wrong choice – of choosing to act badly and to reject God – is necessary to the kind of world that makes possible personal growth:

> According to Christianity, the divine purpose for men is not only that they shall freely act rightly towards one another but that they shall also freely enter into a filial personal relationship with God Himself. There is, in other words, a religious as well as an ethical dimension to this purpose. (1978: 72)

Free will is, then, an essential component of a world in which souls can mature.

In regard to natural evil, Hick argues that a world constituted by physical objects operating by stable natural laws is also necessary to a soul-making environment. The physical world provides a context of moral and spiritual life, a world in which both pleasure and pain are possible for sentient creatures so that they will not mistakenly believe that life is a hedonistic paradise. Thus, pain and suffering can prompt human beings to search for deeper meaning and for God.

Much of Hick's argument revolves around the instrumental (teleological) value of evils: both natural and moral evils contribute to the soul-making process. Thus, it seems that a considerable amount of evil may be necessary to an environment that is suited for soul-making. In effect, the identification of the soul-making function of evils seems tantamount to denying that there are gratuitous evils. Yet Hick does consider the haunting question regarding why God allows ostensibly "dysteleological evil" – that is, evils that are excessive and go beyond anything rationally required of a soul-making process:

> Need the world contain the more extreme and crushing evils which it in fact contains? Are not life's challenges often so severe as to be self-defeating when considered as soul-making influences? Man must (let us suppose) cultivate the soil so as to win his bread by the sweat of his brow; but need there be the gigantic famines, for example in China, from which millions have so miserably perished? (1978: 329–30)

Ultimately, Hick appeals to "mystery" because we cannot explain the excess and random character of much evil. But then he presses even dysteleological evil into the service of soul-making theodicy, saying that even the mystery of dysteleological evil has soul-making value. After all, human misery in this world calls forth deep personal sympathy and energetic efforts to help (1978: 334). So, for Hick, there seems to be no gratuitous evil because all evil serves a purpose – which means that Hick essentially denies the factual premise. God permits evil, as Hick explains, to "bring out of it an even greater good than would have been possible if evil had never existed" (1978: 176).

Additional elements of Hick's position include his view of life after death as the continuation of God's plan of soul-making. Since many people suffer and die without achieving moral and spiritual maturity, Hick argues that the soul-making process must be available to them in the afterlife. In fact, Hick postulates that a universal salvation of all humanity is a "practical certainty" as God continues to love and draw humanity into his Kingdom (1978: 334). This affirmation of divine persistence completes the progressive, developmental, and eschatological orientation of Irenaean theodicy. Actually, in rejecting the existence of utterly gratuitous evil, Hick's version of Irenaean theodicy agrees with Augustinian theodicy that "all temporal and therefore finite evils" will be outweighed in the Kingdom of God because it is "an infinite, because eternal, good" (1978: 350)

Leibnizian Theodicy

Gottfried Leibniz argued in his book *Theodicy* from a strong view of omnipotence and omniscience to the conclusion that God cannot be blamed for evil (1952a). Leibniz reasoned that since God is morally perfect, he would want to create the most perfect world from among all logically possible worlds. Further, since God is omniscient, he would know which world is best to actualize by his power. Therefore, this world – the actual world – is the best of all possible worlds (Leibniz 1952b: paras. 30–3).

According to Leibniz, God's goodness, knowledge, and power guarantee that he will select that possible world from among all other alternative worlds that contains the optimum balance of good over evil. Some commentators mistakenly interpret Leibniz to claim that this most perfect world contains the least amount of evil commensurate with there being a world at all. Instead, he is really claiming that that God actualized that possible world containing the least amount of evil necessary to make the world the best world on the whole, acknowledging that some less-than-best worlds also have less evil. Leibniz states, "if the smallest evil that comes to pass in the world were missing in it, it would no longer be this world; which, with nothing omitted and all allowance made, was found the best by the Creator who chose it" (1952b: para. 9). Simply put, all evils contribute to this world's being the best possible: "Not only does [God] derive from [evils] greater goods, but he finds them connected with the greatest goods of all those that are possible: so that it would be a fault not to permit them" (Leibniz 1952b: para. 127). Obviously, some goods are made possible only by the presence of evil. Since compassion is a great value, for example, suffering must be permitted in order to evoke it. Leibniz employs an aesthetic motif, reminiscent of Augustine, indicating that mere quantitative maximalization is dull and uninteresting and that, instead, God allows pain and disorder to elicit richness, quality, and beauty in the world.

A number of critical questions deserve treatment in another venue – for example, whether Leibniz's conception of omnipotence, discussed in Section 3, obviates free will and whether it impugns God's power that he cannot make a better world than this one. For present purposes, however, the net result is that Leibnizian theodicy is tantamount to a denial of the factual premise in the evidential argument by virtue of affirming the evil we have to be indispensable to the greatest possible world. For Leibniz, the denial of gratuitous evil is not an empirical judgment but is instead a strict deduction from a priori assumptions about God's attributes. Further consideration could probe the implication of this view that our world is not capable of improvement, which runs counter to our ordinary moral judgments.

Process Theodicy

Based on the metaphysical vision of Alfred North Whitehead and developed by his intellectual followers such as Charles Hartshorne, process theodicy rejects omnipotence in order to absolve God from blame for evil. In contrast to best-possible-world theodicy, process theodicy does not deny gratuitous evil in the world. Process thinkers reject the strong conception of omnipotence that supports the denial of gratuitous evil and build their theodicy around an alternative conception of divine power, which means that process theodicy is not based on standard theism but on a version of nonstandard theism at best. The metaphysical picture of reality invoked comes from Alfred North Whitehead's view that the essence of reality is *becoming* rather than *being*, a reversal of the traditional approach (1926: 98, 1929: 524–5).

Central to process theodicy is the emphasis on change, development, and evolution – in both the creaturely world and God. Creatures are conscious, ever-changing centers of activity and experience rather than relatively enduring substances (Whitehead 1929: 343). God, according to process thought, has two natures: his Primordial Nature and Consequent Nature. In God's Primordial Nature, he knows all eternal possibilities for how the creaturely world can advance and decides his ideal aims for the unfolding world; God's Consequent Nature contains the actual experiences and responses of creatures from among these possibilities. Thus, God's Consequent Nature changes in response to events in the creaturely world. Indeed, God is in the process of change – not something that classical theists readily accept. Process theism is often labeled "panentheism," which means that the experiences of the world are somehow included in God (Peterson 1987: 123).

For process thought, God is not "infinite in power" and has no "monopoly on power," contrary to many traditional theisms. Since finite creatures are also centers of power (or "freedom" or "self-determination"), they can bring about new states of affairs that God cannot control. Although standard theisms typically claim that God bestows some degree of significant freedom on creatures, process thought holds that freedom – the power of self-determination – is inherent in each individual. Charles Hartshorne and other process theists maintain that God has all the power that it is possible for a being to have but not all the power that there is (Hartshorne 1945: 545ff, 1984: 11ff). Process thinker David Ray Griffin states that God cannot eliminate evil because "God cannot unilaterally effect any state of affairs" (1976: 280). Yet, while God's power is not coercive, it is persuasive in seeking to "lure" or "urge" creatures toward the good.

In the evolving world, when negative ("evil") experiences occur and threaten to thwart the divine aim, God tries to persuade creatures toward new ideal possibilities. So goes the world process as God continually seeks to bring increased order and significance out of aboriginal chaos and triviality. According to process theodicists, God's goal for the universe is the maximization of value in the experience of creaturely realities, even when evil is an ineliminable part of their experience. Although process metaphysics holds that finite creatures are always perishing with no prospect of individual immortality, process theodicy affirms that God fittingly remembers their experiences – conferring on them "objective immortality" (Hartshorne 1962: 262). Thus, "the Kingdom of Heaven" is simply God's own synthesis of all earthly experiences – but not a rectification of all evils.

At this point, we can make several observations about process theism and its implications for theodicy. Clearly, process theism challenged the strong theistic concept of divine power in relation to creaturely freedom (Peterson 1987: 121–39), leading some theists to argue that an oversimplified "either/or" distinction between coercive and persuasive power is inadequate because there are various modes of divine power – such as "productive power" or "sustaining power" or "enabling power" – many of which are compatible with moral persuasion (Frankenberry 1981: 181–4). Also, some commentators question whether an essentially aesthetic solution to the problem of evil (in God's fitting remembrance of creaturely experiences) is adequate when the problem is fundamentally about God's moral goodness. Regarding gratuitous evil, it is difficult to think of another tradition in theodicy that squares up more explicitly with apparently gratuitous evils, but it does this at the cost of surrendering standard theism. The question for more mainline theists, then, is whether there might be an interpretation of divine power and other attributes that allows for the possibility of genuinely gratuitous evil – a matter we explore in Section 6.

Alvin Plantinga's Felix Culpa Theodicy

In contemporary discussions, various important theodicies have been advanced, two of which we will now compare and contrast. A theodicy offered by Alvin Plantinga departed from his usual defensive approach in arguing that evil contributes to the overall goodness and value of the world. Marilyn Adams advanced a response to evil that specifically explores how God can deal with particularly extreme cases of suffering and devastation in the lives of individuals.

Plantinga's contribution became known as Felix Culpa Theodicy, which is a version of greater-good theodicy. Sidestepping Rowe's stipulation that the discussion include only the resources of RST (restricted standard theism), Plantinga includes the Christian doctrines of Incarnation and Atonement in his theodicy (2004: 1–25). His aim is to identify and describe some very great goods that God could not have achieved in the created world without permitting the evils it actually contains.

In his fascinating piece "Supralapsarianism, or 'O Felix Culpa,'" Plantinga contends that it is possible that God's intention in creation was to actualize (weakly actualize) a really good possible world (2004: 5–6). Understand "weak actualization" as bringing about everything else in the world except the actions of libertarian free creatures, which complete the world (Plantinga 1985: 49). The value of possible worlds depends on the value of the states of affairs they include: John's being in pain is bad while John's suffering magnificently is good; there being many people acting in love toward each other is good while there being people who hate God and each other is bad; and so on. The total values of possible worlds can be ranked in terms of the balance of good-making qualities they contain – such as happiness, beauty, justice, and love of God, on the one hand – and bad-making characteristics – such as suffering, pain, sin, and rejection of God, on the other hand. Careful reflection on theistic belief provides a way of thinking about the value of possible worlds. For one thing, if God's existence is necessary, then he exists in all possible worlds; and theism entails that God himself is infinitely valuable. So there are no possible worlds in which God does not exist, and any world God chooses for weak actualization will necessarily contain the great-making characteristic of God's own infinite value. Of course, the possible world consisting in God alone existing would also be very good.

Furthermore, reflection on distinctively Christian theistic belief, according to Plantinga, extends our thinking about the value of worlds. Given the traditional concept of God as essentially perfect in goodness, knowledge, and power, it follows that the world God has created is very good and that there are no worlds he would have created that are less than very good. Of course, we can in some sense imagine worlds in which all persons are always in excruciating pain, but no such worlds are in fact possible if God is a necessary and perfect being. Thus, it follows that all possible worlds that God creates are very good. But this does not mean that even a world W in which God alone exists is of maximal value such that no possible worlds are better than W. A world that also contains free creatures who always do what is right would perhaps be a better world than W. This is true even if we grant that the good of God's existence is incommensurable with both creaturely goods and evils. So it still follows that every possible world is a very good world.

However, some good possible worlds are much more valuable than others. Our world and some other possible worlds contain a significant contingent good-making feature: the towering good of divine Incarnation and Atonement. Plantinga follows Christian doctrine in stating that God in Christ, the Second Person of the Trinity, became incarnate in Jesus of Nazareth, lived a holy and sinless life, and suffered and died for sinful human beings, providing reconciliation to the Father. Plantinga asks rhetorically, "Could there be a display of love to rival this?" Then he adds, "More to the present purpose, could there be a good-making feature of a world to rival this?" (2004: 7). Plantinga maintains that this good is so clearly incomparably great, displaying the matchless beauty of self-sacrificing love, that any world with it is better than any without it (or at least without some similar divine initiative).

So any world with Incarnation and Atonement contains two infinite goods: the good of God's existence and the good of Incarnation and Atonement. At this point, Plantinga articulates what he calls "the strong value assumption" (2004: 10):

> A: There is a level L of excellence among possible worlds such that all the worlds at that level or above contain Incarnation and Atonement.

Plantinga mentions that his ensuing argument would work on a more modest assumptions, but let us here follow his line of thought on the strong value assumption. Now, according to Plantinga, if God intends to actualize a really good possible world, one whose value exceeds L, he will create a world containing Incarnation and Atonement. But all worlds containing Incarnation and Atonement also contain evil, since the presence of sin and evil is a necessary condition of Atonement. Hence, all of the really good worlds – with a level of excellence L or higher – contain Incarnation, Atonement, sin, suffering, and evil.

For Plantinga, we now have a Christian theodicy explaining why there is all the evil in the actual world – that is, showing why evil is necessary to a greater good: it is because God wanted to create a highly valuable world, one that contained Incarnation and Atonement, but all highly valuable worlds, therefore, also contain evil. Plantinga quotes the famous line from the Easter Vigil *Exultet*: *O felix culpa quae talem et tantum meruit habere redemptorem*, which translates "O happy fault that merited such and so great a Redeemer." Plantinga explains that Adam's sin is considered fortunate (*"O Felix Culpa!"*) because it necessitated Christ's redeeming work. Surprisingly, then, sin and evil occasion the highest possible good. Essentially, Plantinga's claim is that suffering is part of an excellent world.

Of course, we might probe *felix culpa* theodicy and ask whether, paradoxically, the value of God's redeeming activity is so great that it is worth breaking relation with God on purpose so that God can restore it. Something in this claim may seem mistaken:

> If humanity had not fallen, then this world would not be a really good world with a level of excellence of L or above.

After all, an unfallen world that includes freely chosen relationship with God would actually be the fulfilment of God's original purpose in creation (John Paul II 1997: 9). Probing *felix culpa* theodicy from another angle, it could be supposed that, since Christianity affirms that God is a self-revealing God, the great good of Incarnation might be quite likely even in an unfallen world because God would still want to display how close he wants to be with humanity. Indeed, Christianity entails that the Incarnation even in a possible unfallen world would still reveal God's same self-giving love demonstrated by Incarnation and Atonement in the actual fallen world. Pursuing this line of thinking further, it is difficult to avoid the conclusion that, in Christian terms, it was always possible, and always more desirable, for sin not to occur (Peterson 2008: 183–5).

Marilyn Adams's Response to Horrendous Evils

Marilyn Adams provides a distinctively Christian response to severe evil in the world that she officially frames as a defense, but her response lends itself to further theodical reflections – hence, its inclusion in this section. Adams explicitly rejects greater-good theodicies such as Plantinga's, which she calls "generic and global," or world-level theodicies. According to Adams, discussions of evil are typically conducted at too high a level of abstraction and revolve around whether standard theism can provide reasons why the world is good on balance in spite of the evils it contains. Adams the Christian thinker also agrees with other monotheistic traditions that suffering and evil for some individuals is connected to their overall good by making possible depth of character, clearer understanding of God, and the like. By contrast, she emphasizes concrete and specific evils occurring at the individual level that are so serious that they threaten to destroy the value and meaning of the life of the individual person who participates in them. What she calls "horrendous evils" are such that no finite good, secular or religious, can defeat them (Adams 1990: 218).

Following Adams, a more technical definition of "horrendous evil" can be extracted from her writing:

> "Evil *e* is horrendous" if and only if "participation in *e* by person *p* (by doing or suffering *e*) constitutes *prima facie* reason to doubt whether *p*'s life could (given *e*) be a great good to *p* on the whole." (1990: 211–12)

Adams's paradigmatic examples of such evils include the following:

> the rape of a woman and axing off of her arms, psycho-physical torture whose ultimate goal is the disintegration of personality, betrayal of one's deepest loyalties, child abuse of the sort described by Ivan Karamazov, child pornography, parental incest, slow death by starvation, the explosion of nuclear bombs over populated areas. (1999: 26)

Such evils raise the question of whether such persons' lives can be a great good to them.

Utilizing Roderick Chisholm's distinction between *balancing off* (when mutually opposing parts of a whole cancel each other) and *defeat* (when some organic unity among the values of parts and whole transcends the disvalue of some part) (1968), Adams speaks of the need for positive, decisive defeat of horrendous evil. Since no finite good or set of goods could defeat horrendous evils, Adams argues that only the infinite good of God himself as conceived by the Christian tradition can defeat horrendous evils (1999: 26-30). Her further description of the horror-defeating goodness of God draws on Christology regarding God's incarnation in Christ, whose voluntary self-defilement leads to holiness. By identification with this self-sacrificing holiness, participants in horrors can find meaning and value in their lives; some find it in this life, but all are assured of it in the life to come. Thus, in Adams's theodicy, the important kind of "goodness" God displays is "goodness to individual persons" – which, unlike world-level theodicies, meets Rowe's Person-Centered Requirement (1999: 31).

We cannot continue here the study of various types of theodicies but rather leave that task to the interested reader (see McBrayer and Howard-Snyder 2013; Meister and Moser 2017). Monotheisms generally endorse the quest for an adequate theoretical theodicy for evil but also rely on their less systematic scriptures, wisdom teachings, and practical admonitions regarding how to engage evil.

5 Evil in Monotheistic Scriptures, Theologies, and Practices

Each monotheism draws responses to evil from its scriptures, wisdom litera-tures, and practical teachings. Many themes identified at the theoretical level in the previous section are found in primary religious sources but in less systemat-ically developed form. Surveying themes in these religious materials provides a sense of the distinctiveness of how each monotheistic religion engages suffering and evil, including how it directs the spiritual life of believers in a world that includes evil. In fact, according to some thinkers, religious responses are more authentic because classical Greek ideas taint the philosoph-ical concept of God.

Greek Influence in the Problem of Evil

Objections to the influence of Greek ideas of divine perfection and immut-ability on religious issues, including the problem of evil, are worth noting. In Christian thought, such objections are readily found. Theologian Tertullian asked rhetorically, "What has Jerusalem to do with Athens?" (1722: chap. 7). To describe his powerful religious experience, Blaise Pascal penned the following words: "Fire. The God of Abraham, the God of Isaac, the God of Jacob, and not of the philosophers and men of science" (1966: 309ff). More recently, open theists have critiqued the classical theistic concept of God, which is involved in the problem of evil and standard responses to it, as hopelessly flawed by its roots in Greek philosophy (Pinnock 1994). These kinds of perspectives insist on the incompatibility between the God of living faith and the God of classical theism, which is seen as a hybrid construct, an uncomfortable amalgam (Harnack 1958).

Of course, thinkers who discredit philosophical engagement with religious ideas are historically in the minority while the majority embraces philosophy to assist in our understanding and systematization of the concept of God. Indeed, numerous monotheistic thinkers comprehensively apply Greek philosophy to theology – for example, see the works of Jewish thinker Saadia Gaon (2011), Muslim thinker Ibn Rushd, known in the West as Averroes (2001), and Christian thinker Thomas Aquinas (1920). Aquinas explicitly argues that faith and reason are harmonious, that theology and philosophy have a symbiotic relationship, and that theism provides the framework for a great synthesis of all knowledge.

Regarding the problem of evil specifically, Greek thought leads to a concept of God as a self-existent unity that is timeless, immutable, and impassible – properties that are difficult to square with properties of compassion and mercy (see Sanders 1994: 59–100). This concept of God generates questions about why God's temporal, mutable creation, for which God alone is responsible, contains evil. For another thing, Greek ideas of divine perfection imply that God possesses attributes of power, knowledge, and goodness to a maximal degree – again, raising questions regarding how evil could exist in the created universe. We cannot settle the controversy over the degree to which Greek elements distort or help clarify aspects of God's nature but simply proceed with this background awareness (Bray 1983).

Suffering and Evil in Judaism

Nachmanidies, a thirteenth-century Jewish rabbi and scholar, stated that the problem of suffering and evil is "the most difficult matter, which is at the root both of faith and of apostasy, with which scholars of all ages, people and tongues have struggled" (Sherwin 1988: 960). Perhaps predictably, Jewish thinkers echo many of the general monotheistic themes about evil – including suffering and evil as punishment for sin, as character building, and as opportunity to increase faith. Scholar Yaakov Elman states that trial (Hebrew: *nissayon*) is another important theme (1999: 155–212). In addition to common themes, Jewish theodicy also employs distinctive themes drawn from the Hebrew Bible, Talmud, and Midrash as well as from medieval and modern Jewish thinkers on the subject.

Further contextualization requires placement of the problem of suffering within Jewish history and experience. Extremely important is the covenant between God and the Jewish people given to Abraham (Gen. 15:1–17), which frames Jewish consciousness and raises the question of why God has apparently broken his covenant many times as Jewish communities have suffered greatly. Thus, Judaism faces both the general problem of suffering and evil and its own specific problem. In addition to searching for answers at the theoretical level, Judaism engages suffering and evil at a practical level, particularly pertaining to how religious believers experience and respond to suffering and evil.

While Christian theodicies explicitly strive for comprehensiveness, coherence, and explanatory adequacy, many Jewish theodicies are implicit and unsystematic, often buried in stories, anecdotes, and cryptic statements. The first theme deserving comment pertains to just retribution: the principle that a just God rewards good deeds and punishes evil deeds. The theme of retribution receives critical attention and debate in key Jewish sources. Although a rabbi in the Midrash, for instance, essentially states that "there is no death without sin, no suffering without transgression," the Talmudic deliberations reject this view (Babylonian Talmud, Shabbat 55a). Of course, since human experience contains ample counterevidence to just retribution in temporal life, eschatological interpretations became favored. When Rabbi Jacob learned of a child who fell from a ladder and died while fulfilling two commandments, he commented that "the reward for a commandment is not found in this world" (Babylonian Talmud, Kiddushin 39b).

Future-oriented interpretations, however, still fail to answer all questions. Classic Jewish sources ask, "Why do the wicked prosper and the righteous suffer?" In Ecclesiastes, for example, pessimism leads to the supposition that both the righteous and the wicked ultimately receive the same fate and concludes that there is no perfect justice (9:2). Philosopher Peter van Inwagen clarifies that this is more a problem about justice than a problem about the existence of suffering per se (2006). Nevertheless, the problem of inequitable treatment in Judaism is a subset of the larger problem of evil.

The book of Job wages a sustained attack on the principle of retribution (Glatzer 2002: 2, 74, 287). The book portrays the gripping drama of a righteous man struggling with the Deuteronomic code, which taught that, if a person is righteous, then that person will receive health, wealth, and progeny. Job faithfully obeyed God's laws and yet experiences great misfortune, losing his health, wealth, and progeny. Job is deeply puzzled and bemoans his dire circumstances; his friends arrive to give comfort but quickly turn to blaming him. Three friends plus a younger man repeatedly batter Job with the entrenched principle that God rewards righteousness and punishes wickedness – endorsing what scholars call an "act-consequence paradigm." One friend sarcastically asks Job, "Whoever suffered being righteous?" (Job 4:7) – expressing the conviction that there is no innocent suffering. Job adamantly defends himself against the accusations, arguing both that God is just and that he is innocent of any wrongdoing. Thus, in the Hebrew Bible, Job is the epitome of the righteous sufferer.

For the friends, perfectly just retribution made the triad of God's justice, Job's innocence, and Job's suffering impossible – thus Job's innocence must be denied in order to preserve God's justice in light of Job's obvious suffering. By contrast, Job believed that the triad must hold – but this meant pressing for a conception of divine justice far beyond simplistic legal formulas. The climax of the book is a theophany in which God speaks to Job out of a great Whirlwind, poetically describing the vastness and complexity of God's governance of the world. Indeed, the Whirlwind explicitly rejects the friends' claim that there is no innocent suffering: "You have spoken of me what is false" (Job 42:7). In dismissing the retribution model, the book raises the question of why a person, such as Job, would serve God when circumstances are not favorable. Matitiahu Tsevat explains that this is really a problem about piety, which goes to the deeper nature of faith (1966: 73–106).

Medieval Jewish philosopher Saadiah Gaon (alternatively called al-Fayyumi) argued that God's perfect justice demands an afterlife in which virtue is rewarded and innocent suffering is requited but adds that suffering in this life can be a spiritual correction. Therefore, all who suffer should examine their ways and improve their lives. In *The Book of Theodicy*, Saadiah interprets Job's suffering as a trial of a righteous person to test and purify him (al-Fayyumi 1988: 382–3). Lenn Goodman discusses the rabbinic doctrine of the "tribulations of love" – which is the idea that "God lays unmerited sufferings on those he especially loves to justify enhancing their reward in the hereafter" (2017: 197).

David Shatz observes that tribulations-of-love theories are versions of "soul-making theodicy," a theme also found in Christian and Muslim thought. For Jewish thinkers such as Moses Maimonides, God may permit sufferings, say, that come because of the operation of natural laws, but it is still an opportunity for free response to God (1904). Acceptance of suffering as spiritual therapy is seen in Rabbd Akiva, who while awaiting execution by Roman authorities for teaching the Torah, expressed joy for the opportunity to fulfill the command, "Love God with all of your soul" (Jerusalem Talmud, *Sotah* 5:5). Shatz states that the soul-making explanation of suffering is an "axiological shift" theodicy that moves the person's attention from material circumstances to opportunity to grow in relationship to God (2013: 314).

Any discussion of Jewish theodicy must include the Holocaust, which deeply impacted Jewish thought. Most post-Holocaust Jewish thinkers insist that pre-Holocaust theodicies provide generalizations about suffering and evil that fail to account for the Holocaust as a unique event of great communal suffering requiring a unique explanation – which, unfortunately, is not available. Punishment is not a credible explanation, particularly due to the countless innocent children murdered. Soul-making theodicy is not a satisfying answer because many lives were extinguished without opportunity for spiritual improvement. Appeals to an afterlife in which suffering can retrospectively be considered worth it pale in light of the Holocaust's nearly unimaginable horror in this life.

In the absence of being able to make sense of the Holocaust, some important Jewish thinkers adopted an atheistic stance, as theologian Eugene Borowitz explains:

> Any God who could permit the Holocaust, who could remain silent during it, who could "hide His face" while it dragged on, was not worth believing in. There might well be a limit to how much we could understand about Him, but Auschwitz demanded an unreasonable suspension of understanding. In the face of such great evil, God, the good and the powerful, was too inexplicable, so men said, "God is dead." (1973: 99).

A long history of suffering is a significant factor in the phenomenon of Jewish atheism. Yet, since being Jewish is an ethnic as well as a religious matter, atheism does not necessitate the rejection of Jewish observance and heritage (see Haaretz 2012).

Probably no contemporary Jewish thinker has represented the Jewish problem with God more powerfully than Nobel Peace Prize recipient Elie Wiesel, a survivor of Auschwitz and Buchenwald, infamous Nazi concentration and death camps. Although many readers of his first book, *Night*, viewed it as a rejection of God, Wiesel states that he "never divorced God" but was, and still is, "angry at God" (Wiesel: 1958). Because he believes in God, Wiesel explains, he can quarrel with God (Tippett and Wiesel 2012). Wiesel wrote a play – entitled *The Trial of God* – which was inspired by an event he witnessed as a boy in Auschwitz when three great Jewish scholars debated the case against God for allowing Jewish people to suffer persecution and destruction throughout history.

Examining the play further reveals Wiesel's poignant approach. The setting of the play is seventeenth-century Shamgorod, Poland, at the time of the pogroms, which were organized massacres of Jews. The figure of Berish, who stands vicariously for Wiesel, charges God with hostility, cruelty, and indifference. Witnesses are called, evidence produced, and conclusions drawn, all of which supported a unanimous negative verdict – but there was no time to pronounce it because the pogrom got there first. At the actual trial that Wiesel directly observed at Auschwitz, a clear verdict was reached: the Lord, Creator of Heaven and Earth, is *guilty* of crimes against humanity. Wiesel reports that, after the verdict, a deep silence pervaded the group, and then he heard a rabbi call for evening prayers, and all present recited the Maariv, the evening service (Wiesel recorded by Brown 1979: loc. 42–248). Here we see the profoundly complex psychological dynamics involved in both condemning God and seeking relationship with God.

To this day, the Holocaust is a major factor in Jewish thinking about God – a subject discussed in *(God) After Auschwitz* by Zachary Braiterman (1999).

Indeed, the Holocaust stands as a general symbol of unthinkable evil in theistic attempts at theodicy such that it can be thought to defeat, at the least, particularly Jewish theodicy.

Suffering and Evil in Christianity

The Christian Bible and the creeds assert that Jesus is significant to the problem of evil. As a Jew, Jesus interpreted the Torah and the Prophets in a unique way, teaching that his own life and ministry were about what Judaism "should be" or what trajectory it should be on. In fact, he presented himself as the fulfillment of the Law and the Prophets. Exploring how Jesus related to evil and suffering provides an understanding of how Christian biblical and theological thinking on the problem of evil.

Jesus rejected the retributive theme by decoupling sin from suffering. Regarding those who died in the collapse of an aqueduct system, he remarked, "those eighteen who died when the tower in Siloam fell on them – do you think they were more guilty than all the others living in Jerusalem? I tell you, no!" (Luke 13:1–5). He taught that, regardless of circumstances, persons should repent and come into relationship with God. Jesus consistently emphasized that mercy should be extended to all who suffer. His parable of the Good Samaritan actually exposes the spiritual bankruptcy of external religious righteousness and instead accents mercy: two religious leaders pass by a man at the side of the road who was robbed and beaten by thieves while a Samaritan man who comes along has compassion and helps him (Luke 10:25–37).

Historical Christianity believes that Jesus himself is the ultimate answer to evil, including death. The New Testament records that during his ministry Jesus raised some people from the dead. According to one report, he raised Jairus's daughter, who had just died (Mark 5:21–43). In another report, Jesus raised his friend Lazarus, who had died four days earlier. Just before raising Lazarus, Jesus proclaimed, "I am the resurrection and the life," identifying himself as the one who will eventually transform physical death into eternal life (John 11:25).

The Christian community sees the narrative of Jesus's own unjustified suffering and crucifixion as well as his resurrection and ascension as winning the final victory over suffering and evil. Christians see themselves as participating in that victory, which gives existential hope as well as moral and spiritual power to resist evil and help a suffering world. One New Testament theme is that to suffer persecution for the cause of Christ is a reason for rejoicing because the believer thereby identifies with Christ's suffering and triumph, another variant of the idea that suffering can be beneficial.

Another theme in Christian theology is that Jesus's suffering and death provides a glimpse into the self-sacrificial love of God. Much modern theology has shifted away from the patristic model of God's impassibility to the idea that God suffers with and for the world and is thus to some extent passible, able to feel the infirmities of creatures. Protestant theologians taking this line include Karl Barth (1957), Jürgen Moltmann (1974), and Wolfhart Pannenberg (1973); Catholic theologians would be Hans Urs von Balthasar (1994), Hans Küng (1987), and Marcel Sarot (1992).

While the Christian New Testament explicitly portrays Jesus's confrontation with sin, suffering, and evil, the Old Testament, which is composed of scriptures shared with Judaism, is interpreted as preparatory to the New. For instance, the Genesis story of sin entering the world via Adam and Eve is accompanied by God's promise to send a descendant of Eve who will right the world again, a person Christians take to be Jesus (Gen. 3:1–24). The book of Job is seen by some to anticipate that Jesus would come as the truly righteous sufferer. The book of Isaiah pictures "the suffering servant," who "was wounded for our transgressions" and "by whose wounds we are healed" (Isa. 53:5). Theologian N. T. Wright asserts that Jesus as the suffering servant will bring justice:

> God's justice is not simply a blind dispensing of rewards for the virtuous and punishments for the wicked, though plenty of those are to be found on the way. God's justice is a saving, healing, restorative justice, because the God to whom justice belongs is the Creator God who has yet to complete his original plan for creation and whose justice is designed not simply to restore balance to a world out of kilter but to bring to glorious completion and fruition the creation, teeming with life and possibility, that he made in the first place.
>
> (Wright 2012: 64)

For Christian faith, then, the life, work, and ministry of Jesus is, then, the basis for his bringing about the ultimate redemption and consummation of a good but suffering creation.

Suffering and Evil in Islam

The Qur'an and a generous number of hadiths speak frequently about the facts of suffering and evil. The Qu'ran asks, "Did you suppose that you would go to Paradise untouched by the suffering which was endured by those before you?" (Qur'an 2.214). From the fragility of life in the desert to persecution for the faith, and from pain and grief to injustice, Islam frankly acknowledges the realities of suffering. From this starting point, different Islamic traditions draw out their own themes for understanding these negative phenomena, themes that have counterparts in the other monotheisms.

First, the theme of retribution occurs in the Qur'an and runs through many Islamic explanations of suffering. The Qur'an typically links suffering – by earthquakes, floods, and famines – to human moral and spiritual failings (Michel 2010). In contrast to the influential Augustinian perspective in Christianity, there is no claim that pain and suffering in the world results from the disobedience of a first couple whose sin and guilt are passed down generationally. Concepts of retribution, of course, are ineluctably tied to the idea of just recompense: that the suffering is deserved.

However, apparently undeserved suffering creates further challenges for Islamic thought. Although all monotheisms raise questions of the unmerited and unrequited suffering of innocents and even employ some common themes in response, Islam develops these themes in particular ways. Thus, a second general theme in the Qur'an is that virtue is not always rewarded temporally but is ultimately rewarded in the afterlife. Rumi, the famous Muslim poet, invokes the afterlife idea by employing the image of earthly hardships as the world's "birth pangs" awaiting deliverance (Arberry 1961: 33). Interestingly, an extension of this concept, which is not uncommon in Jewish and Christian thought, is that the bliss of heaven will actually wash away memories of earthly suffering. One hadith attributes the following words to Mohammed:

> The man who had suffered most in the world is brought, and it is said: "Dip him into Heaven for one instant!" Then he is asked: "Have you ever experienced any suffering?" and he replies, "No." (qtd. in Winter 2017: 237)

A slightly different Islamic approach is that sufferings will be remembered in heaven but will be seen from a positive perspective not available in earthly life (al-Ghazālī 1989: 200–1).

A third theme builds on the meaning of the word *muslim*: "to be resigned" – that is, to be totally surrendered to Allah. The Muslim mindset is that hardships and pains must be faithfully endured. Developed along ascetic lines, distress is taken as indicating divine favor, a divine gift to purify the soul. The devotionalistic Sufi tradition, for example, teaches that true spirituality accepts pain, suffering, and hardship as coming from God, who is worthy of love and trust. Timothy Winter notes that the birth-pang idea can apply to each individual:

> Characteristic, then, of the Qur'an's soteriology is its construction of episodes of suffering which, when bravely borne, lead to a wholly unexpected and miraculous outcome: like Mary's parturitive agonies they invite an attitude of resignation and are to be read as unmerited and mysterious foretellings and therefore acts of grace. (2017: 233)

The faithful Muslim may not be able to discern a wonderful divine plan while enduring suffering because it is yet to be manifested.

Deeply rooted in the Qur'an is a fourth and closely related theme pertaining to innocent suffering as a test or trial:

> And We will surely test you with something of fear and hunger and a loss of wealth and lives and fruits, but give good tidings to the patient, Who, when disaster strikes them, say, "Indeed we belong to Allah, and indeed to Him we will return." (Qur'an 2:155–156; 67:2)

This is an Islamic version of soul-making theodicy: the idea that creation is a soul-making environment in which character is both revealed and constructed (Qur'an 18:7; 76:2). For example, pain, suffering, and hardship may inculcate humility or a penitential attitude and thereby build faith (Jackson 2014: 112). An ascetic interpretation is that painful experiences keep the believer's attention on Allah and thus aid the soul's ascent. Of course, familiar criticisms of soul-making theodicy recur in this context: that the degree of involuntary suffering is very often not calibrated to the development of any particular spiritual benefit; that the amount of suffering is sometimes too much for some persons and crushes rather than builds their souls; that young children who suffer intensely or die prematurely are in no credible process of soul-making; and that nonhuman animals that suffer are not participating in a soul-making process.

An important emphasis in Islam is that the believer has obligations to resist and reduce evil in the world. Actually, physical sickness and disability have traditionally received much attention in Muslim theology and jurisprudence (Ghaly 2010: chap. 4). "Health care," states Earle Waugh, "evolved out of Islamic values [and] led to institutions [such as hospitals and medical schools] for the public good" (1999: 1–22). Even if cases of suffering or disability could be interpreted as punishment or test, a Muslim's duty is, nevertheless, to alleviate such evils.

Interestingly, all three monotheistic religions affirm God's infinite wisdom, justice, love, and power, but prioritizes and nuances the divine attributes, creating differences in theoretical understanding and practical response. Judaism historically takes the problem to be primarily about God's justice; Christianity takes it to be essentially about God's love. However, Islam traditionally takes the problem to be about God's power and control – in effect, God's sovereignty. For Judaism the pressing question is about the apparently unjust distribution of the benefits and burdens of life while for Christianity it is about the apparent absence of God's loving purposes in the variable circumstances of human affairs. In Islam the major question is very much about how a strong concept of divine control – in relation to the other divine attributes – can be reconciled with suffering and evil.

Islamic thought contains three main approaches that differ in terms of which attribute is emphasized and how the all attributes are thought to be related. Some Ash'ari thinkers of the medieval period took the first approach, which accents divine power, including his power over good and evil. Abū al-Ḥasan al-Ash'arī made this point in the tenth century:

> [T]here is not good nor evil on earth, save what God wills and . . . things exist
> by God's will . . . not a single person has the capacity to do anything until God
> causes him to act . . . [T]here is no creator save God and the works of human
> beings are things created and decreed by God. (1940: 50–1)

Emphasis on God's power is a form of theological voluntarism that affirms God's right to act as he pleases, including causing events perceived as evil, because there are no independent objective moral facts that God must recognize. One implication is that God is the ultimate cause of human actions, which requires a compatibilist concept of human free will (Qur'an 37:96).

A second approach, mostly taken by representatives of the Mu'tazili and al-Ash'arī schools, moved theodicy away from exclusive focus on divine power and emphasized God's justice. The Mu'tazili position emphasized God's oneness metaphysically and justice as God's essence, such that justice forms the basis of God's acts (Khadduri 1984: 44–5). Typically, the concept of justice here is thought to be common between divine and human, as Imām Ja'far al-Ṣādiq stated in the eighth century: "Justice in the case of God means that you should not ascribe anything to God that if you were to do it would cause you to be blamed and reproached" (Fyzee 1942: 70). Similarly, Sayyid Mujtaba Musavi Lari remarked, "When we see that God is just, it means that His all-knowing and creative essence does nothing that is contrary to wisdom and benefit" (2003: 134).

Muslim thinker Daud Rahbar states that God's justice, not God's power, is the dominant theme of the Qur'an. Thus, theodicy must protect God's justice: "God Himself exercises self-restraint from evil and thus limits His own power. To know Him as a moral Being in Qur'anic terms we must know Him as such, and not as a Force 'let loose'" (qtd. in Otten 1985: 10). Now, the claim that God limits his own power to make room for human responsibility for good or evil comes close to affirming incompatibilist free will. A concept of incompatibilist free will actually helps make sense of reward and punishment according to God's justice and provides theodicy with another element. In any event, if God's morality and justice may be known by humans, if only imperfectly, then the enterprise of theodicy is legitimate.

Taking the idea of divine justice to the extreme, some Muslim thinkers concluded that God must have created the best of all possible worlds.

Eleventh-century al-Ghazālī, who is associated with the Ashʿarite school, wrote, "there is in possibility nothing more wondrous [and perfect] than what is" (1990: 13:2515–18). Indeed, for al-Ghazālī, the world is formed "according to the necessarily right order, in accord with what must be and as it must be and in the measure in which it must be" (Ormsby 1984: 326). Thus, on this view, the world cannot be better than it is, a position advanced, as we saw in Section 4, by the Christian thinker Leibniz (2020).

Between these two approaches that are based on power and justice, respectively, a third approach was developed, an intermediate view that balanced God's power and justice. Medieval Muslim theologians and legal experts, many Sufis and Ashʿaris, and numerous modern Muslim scholars endorse this approach (see al-Sharabāṣī 1956; al-Shaʿrāwī 1995: 58–9; al-Zamīlī 1988). According to this group, the Qur'anic pattern is to integrate the divine names for the attributes of omnipotence, justice, and wisdom to provide a more complete view of God. For instance, the Qur'an uses "the Powerful" (*Al-ʿAzīz*) eleven times with "the Merciful" (*Al-Raḥīm*) and twenty-nine times with "the All-Wise" (*Al-Ḥakīm*). The balanced approach rejected both the Muʿtazili accent on retributive justice that is assessable by human standards and the Ashʿaris accent on pure voluntaristic power as inadequate for Islamic theodicy (Hoover 2007: 270–84). The balanced approach emphasized that all events are redeemable, although human rationality may not always be able to discern God's purposes in them. Under the constraint that God is never to be blamed for evil events, many familiar themes in theodicy can be developed (Ghaly 2014: 147–72).

Anti-Theodicy

Although monotheisms contain elements that support the project of theodicy, they also contain some elements that diminish or reject theodicy. Four different approaches to "anti-theodicy" can be identified in the three monotheisms – that theodicy is *impossible, irreverent, irrelevant*, and *insulting*. The position that theodicy is impossible generally appeals to the perceived gap between human and divine. The view that theodicy is irreverent makes it a spiritual fault for finite humans to question the infinite God. The view that theodicy is irrelevant characteristically cites something of greater comparative value than rational theodicy, such as personal experience of God or practical response to evil. Accusations that theodicy is insulting to the sufferer contend that rational explanation tends to justify the status quo and to silence or minimize the sufferer.

In Judaism, we can find the idea that theodicy is impossible because God is Wholly Other, evading human categories. In *Guide to the Perplexed*, Maimonides explains that there is "nothing in common" between God and any other being, including human beings (1904: 52, 247). Since this position entails that we cannot know or speak of God, Maimonides advocates a *via negativa* approach that allows humans to say only what God is not, but not what God is, which thus preempts positive explanation of evil.

The idea that theodicy is irreverent is not uncommon in Jewish thought. Zophar accuses Job of blasphemy for questioning God regarding suffering: "Can you fathom the mysteries of God? Can you probe the limits of the Almighty?" (Job 11).

Judaism also contains the perspective that theodicy is irrelevant. Usually, direct experience of the divine is considered far more valuable than rational understanding of God. Jewish mystics and others often claim that their trust in God is based in a compelling experience or a choice made in faith. In Martin Buber's terms, an "I-Thou" personal relationship with God trumps intellectual understanding. Jewish philosopher Howard Wettstein argues that the philosophical problem of evil is conditioned by Greek concepts, which are alien to Jewish religious understanding, and is thus irrelevant (1999: 115–25).

Among post-Holocaust Jewish thinkers, the charge is often made that theodicy is insulting to those who suffer. Carved into the prison cell walls of Mauthausen concentration camp in Austria are the following words: *Wenn es einen Gott gibt muß er mich um Verzeihung bitten.* Inscribed by an unknown and long-perished author, these words translate, "If there is a God, He will have to beg my forgiveness" (Lassley 2015: art. 3). Talmud scholar David Weiss-Halivni states that "rationalizations are theologically offensive" because "a justification, by definition, means: it should have happened, it's justice, it's the fitting course of events" (1998: chap. 6). Emil Fackhenheim remarked, "I won't even consider finding a purpose in Auschwitz because the very attempt to find it is blasphemous" (1989: 295). Holocaust theology sees the Holocaust not just as another case of evil to be explained like other evils but as a unique evil of such depth and proportion that it defies explanation.

Strains of anti-theodicy are also found in Islam. For instance, the position that theodicy is impossible is found in various Muslim traditions that teach that God's purposes are unfathomable: "We cannot pass beyond the scope of God's knowledge" (e.g., al-Ashʿarī 1940: 50–1; Rahman 2000: 62). Since God cannot be judged by the same criteria as humans, the problem of evil cannot impugn God. Kenneth Cragg states that God's utter transcendence explains why Islam "does not find a theodicy necessary either for its theology or its worship" (Cragg 1975: 16). Another kind of anti-theodicy is that theodicy is irreverent. The Sunni emphasis on unquestioning surrender to the divine will would support such a view. Quotes from the Qur'an also seem supportive, such as the follow-ing: "He is not asked about what He does; it is [humans] who are asked" (Qur'an 21:23).

Furthermore, since the Qur'an speaks of suffering as necessary to spiritual improvement, an Islamic case could be made that theodicy is irrelevant. Islam's main spiritual and practical objectives are aimed at helping believers overcome various kinds of evils in human experience (Rouzati 2018). Although it is difficult to detect in Muslim thought the claim that theodicy is insulting to the sufferer, the position of Ibn Sīnā (Avicenna) could be interpreted by some as insulting to sufferers because he contends that there is in reality no problem of evil. Agreeing with Ibn Sīnā, the mystic Muhyī al-dīn Ibn al-ʿArabī in the thirteenth century wrote, "Existence in general is purely good and non-existence is purely evil. However, such evil that may exist is imbued with good. . . . The whole world then enjoys complete happiness" (qtd. in Diyāb 2000: 36). Of course, the concern over this kind of all's-well-from-God's-perspective position is that it desensitizes us to the suffering of others and demotivates efforts to help.

Expectedly, the Christian tradition contains anti-theodicy positions similar to those above. For example, the view that theodicy is impossible is entailed by some construals of Skeptical Theism if theodicy is understood as the project of giving plausible reasons for God's permission of evil. As Michael Bergmann says, God's transcendent wisdom leaves finite humans "in the dark" with respect to God-justifying reasons for evils (Bergmann 2001: 289, 291). Also, the view that theodicy is irreverent can be found along the spectrum of Christian thought: critical rational engagement with religion is seen as an arrogant attempt to judge God. Classical Protestantism asserts that sin – understood as "total depravity" – prevents the creature from accurately understanding God's ways. God is exempt from human standards because his voluntaristic sovereignty determines what is right. In Luther's own words, theodicy along with all critical rational investigation of God is blasphemy: "Why do you not restrain yourself, and deter others from prying into these things which God wills should be hidden from us, and which He has not delivered to us in the Scriptures? It is here . . . we are to reverence what lies hidden, to adore the secret counsels of the divine Majesty" (2019: 29).

The idea that theodicy is irrelevant to Christian belief is an implication of a Christian fideist position that values choosing faith over intellectually evalu-ating the rational credentials of Christian belief. Karl Barth, a famous Protestant theologian in the mid-twentieth century, proclaimed that faith is self-validating, both in the believer's experience and in any presentation of the faith to non-believers (1979: 5). In this vein, Barth is reported to have stated, "belief cannot argue with unbelief: it can only preach to it" (Meynell 1998: 125). The irrelevance of philosophical theodicy is also urged by theologian Jürgen Moltmann, whose book *The Crucified God* makes the case that the cross of Christ is emblematic of the theme that God suffers with and for the world. Moltmann writes, "the suffering of abandonment is overcome by the suffering of love, which is not afraid of what is sick and ugly but accepts it and takes it to itself in order to heal it" (2015: 61). Thus, even if a theoretical account of evil has considerable explanatory value, it is beside the most fundamental point.

Christian views that theodicy is insulting to suffers may be found. For instance, British theologian Kenneth Surin follows the theology of the cross represented in Moltmann but urges that theodicy be about alleviating suffering and evil, arguing that theoretical answers for evil are offensive to (and perhaps abusive of) the sufferer by not encouraging efforts to remove the suffering (1986). Theologian Terrence Tilley also denies that the enterprise of theodicy has any positive function and declares that it is actually immoral or "evil" because it "disguises real evils" by making them items of abstract discussion rather than leading others to help those who suffer (1991: 3).

Anti-theodicies characteristically turn on strict dichotomies – philosophical/ theological, rational/existential, theoretical/practical – that are not widely accepted in Christian thought. While some Christian thinkers argue against the enterprise of theodicy, others believe that it aids understanding, accents God's opposition to evil, and even provides context for practical action. To explore further the arguments pro and con regarding the enterprise of theodicy, the interested reader should consult the reference piece "Anti-Theodicy" by Nick Trakakis (2017: 124–42).

6 The Way Forward

For the world's monotheisms, the perennial problem of evil has been a source of great difficulty. Yet, responses to the problem, while greatly varied, yield some important insights that factor into a more adequate approach. Furthermore, related problems discussed in this section – regarding divine hiddenness, divine evil, and the Continental critique of the analytic approach – provide additional insights into the issues impinging on the problem of evil. This section charts a new direction for theistic response to the argument from gratuitous evil by invoking these insights and by situating evil in the context of worldview comparison where theism has notable advantages over naturalism.

The Problem of Divine Hiddenness

The idea of "divine hiddenness" – that God is somehow hidden, absent, or silent – has a long history in religious literature. Although the Apostle Paul stated that God's eternal power and nature "are clearly seen from the things that are made" (Romans 1:20), other biblical literature states that God "hides" or "withdraws" his presence. The book of Isaiah declares, "Truly, you are a God who hides himself"; the Psalmist asks, "Why do you hide your face?" (45:15; see also Psalm 44:23–24). Some theologians speak of *Deus absconditus*, which is Latin for "the God who absconds."

Various explanations for the nonobviousness of God have been offered – for example, that God hides from believers at certain times for specific reasons, perhaps to build their faith. Mystics in all monotheistic traditions share the assumption that the rational apprehension of God's nature is impossible because of his essential otherness but that relationship to God is intimately available through direct experience. However, when God seems absent during times of difficulty or suffering, believers in all theistic traditions give voice to anxiety, doubt, and the desire for a sense of God's presence.

In *Divine Hiddenness and Human Reason*, John Schellenberg formulated an argument for atheism from hiddenness that generated much subsequent discussion, including discussion about its relation to the problem of evil (1993). The hiddenness argument recognizes that some persons are open to a personal relationship with God but still cannot bring themselves to believe that God exists, which is prerequisite to relationship with God. Consider a brief rendition of the argument:

(1) There are people who are capable of relating personally to God but who, through no fault of their own, fail to believe.
[Factual Premise]
(2) If there is an omnipotent, perfectly good, loving God who is always seeking relationship, then there are no such people.
[Theological Premise]
(3) Therefore, there is no omnipotent, perfectly good God.
[Conclusion]

The data set here does not include resistant nonbelief that refuses to see positive evidence or rejects relationship with God; it does include persons who were once believers but lost faith upon further reflection on the evidence. Thus, the argument triggers on fact of "nonresistant nonbelief" or "reasonable nonbelief."

As with the evidential argument from evil, three broad possible types of theistic response are available: reject the factual premise based on some theistic explanation of nonresistant nonbelief; adopt skepticism about the epistemic status of the factual premise; revise the theological premise in favor of a modified understanding of what God would allow. First, some argue that there is no inculpable nonbelief, that nonbelief is somehow due to a blameworthy defect – a move parallel to the view that gratuitous evils do not exist. As one possible explanation for rejecting the factual premise, Daniel Howard-Snyder and Adam Green (2016) suggest the case of the person who is nonresistant for improper prudential motives, such as fear of punishment, which is not conducive to positive relationship. However, it is doubtful that this explanation can cover all cases of nonresistant nonbelief.

Second, skeptical responses to the factual premise argue that humans are not in a position epistemically to tell whether there are good reasons for God to permit reasonable nonbelief. Affirmation of the factual premise assumes that, if there is a good reason for a loving, relational God to be hidden, then we should be able to discern it, whereas skepticism cites our inability to discern it. Again, skepticism seems less effective against the factual premise in the argument from hiddenness than it seems to be against the factual premise in the argument from evil. This is because the straightforward principle that a perfectly good God desires loving relationship leaves much less room for skepticism regarding our noetic grasp of his reasons for declining or postponing such a relationship if available. Robert Adams states the point as follows:

> The ideal of Christian love includes not only benevolence but also desire for certain kinds of personal relationship, for their own sake. Were that not so, it would be strange to call it "love." . . . The Bible depicts a God who seems at least as interested in divine-human relationships as in human happiness per se. (1987: 188–9)

Thus, it seems fundamental that, surely, a perfectly loving personal God would ensure that there is no reasonable or inculpable nonbelief because belief in God's existence is preliminary to entering relationship with God, which is a great good (perhaps the greatest good) for human creatures.

Third, some argue that the theological premise is false or somehow inadequate and thus requires further clarification regarding what a loving God would do or allow in terms of the conditions for belief. Michael Murray echoes John Hick's point that "epistemic distance" is essential to "soul-making." Thus, God should not make his existence too obvious to creatures so as to protect their moral and spiritual freedom; instead, God must make the world religiously ambiguous so as not to coerce the belief of creatures (Murray 2003: loc. 1100; see also Hick 1978: 281). This generous scope of freedom also allows for nonresistant nonbelief that results in persons simply not finding the evidence to be convincing.

A couple observations are in order concerning the relationship between the problem of hiddenness and the problem of evil. First, the problem of hiddenness appears to be a subset of the problem of evil. The premises of the argument from hiddenness do not focus on evil per se but on the phenomenon of reasonable nonbelief itself, which can be viewed as an evil, a serious negative in a supposedly theistic universe. Thus, reasonable nonbelief must go on the long list with many other evils, perhaps as a kind of gratuitous neglect or unfairness on God's part, something God should not let happen if he exists at all. Second, evils, particularly apparently gratuitous evils, support much non-culpable nonbelief by providing evidence against the existence of God.

The Problem of Divine Evil

What is often called "the problem of divine evil" is another challenge to theism based on the morally objectionable divine commands and actions as portrayed in monotheistic scriptures. Although Jewish, Christian, and Islamic scriptures describe God as morally perfect and worthy of obedience, devotion, and worship, some portions of these same scriptures can be seen as depicting God as punitive, wrathful, and tyrannical. Like the problem of divine hiddenness, the problem of divine evil may be viewed as a subset of the problem of evil. The argument is that scriptural passages referring to God's objectionable commands and actions pro-vide the evidence against God's perfect goodness. This difficulty confronts all monotheistic scriptures – including the Christian New Testament and the Qur'an, but it has particularly acquired traction regarding the Hebrew Bible, which Christians accept as their Old Testament and which even Muslims take to be revelation at a certain level. The issues treated here largely deal with problem cases in the Hebrew Bible.

Various passages picture a God who condones, commends, and sometimes commands moral wrongdoing such as genocide, slavery, child sacrifice, and rape. New Atheist Richard Dawkins offers harsh criticism:

> The God of the Old Testament is arguably the most unpleasant character in all fiction [and is] proud of it: A petty, unjust, unforgiving control-freak; a vindictive, blood-thirsty ethnic cleanser; a misogynistic, homophobic, racist, infanticidal, genocidal, filicidal, pestilential, megalomaniacal, sado-masochistic, capriciously malevolent bully. (2006: 51)

The question here is not why a supremely good God would allow evil in his created world; instead, it is whether the God of scripture is himself evil, committing or commanding atrocities that would today be labeled murders, war crimes, genocides, and the like. Any human being or group doing such things would be unequivocally pronounced evil.

We can only briefly survey items on the critics' list of troubling passages. The conquest of Canaan has been particularly controversial and provides a case study. In Deuteronomy, we find the following divine instructions:

When you draw near to a town to fight against it, offer it terms of peace. If it accepts your terms of peace and surrenders to you, then all the people in it shall serve you at forced labor. If it does not submit to you peacefully, but makes war against you, then you shall besiege it; and when the Lord your God gives it into your hand, you shall put all its males to the sword. You may, however, take as your booty the women, the children, livestock, and everything else in the town, all its spoil. You may enjoy the spoil of your enemies, which the Lord your God has given you. Thus you shall treat all the towns that are very far from you, which are not towns of the nations here. But as for the towns of these peoples that the Lord your God is giving you as an inheritance, you must not let anything that breathes remain alive. You shall annihilate them – the Hittites and the Amorites, the Canaanites and the Perizzites, the Hivites and the Jebusites – just as the Lord your God has commanded, so that they may not teach you to do all the abhorrent things that they do for their gods, and you thus sin against the Lord your God. (Deut. 20:10–18)

This passage describes God commanding the enslavement of towns that surrender to the Israelites and the mass slaughter of particular people groups, such as the Hittites and Canaanites. Cyril Rodd states, "The Old Testament can easily appear to be the most bloodthirsty of all sacred scriptures within the great religious traditions" – in fact, "the Old Testament *glories* in war" (2001: 18, 189).

Other kinds of stories also make the critics' list. For example, the story of the binding of Isaac: God commands a specific individual, Abraham, to sacrifice his only son. Louis Antony charges God with giving "a monstrous and utterly outrageous order," and she further points out the total horror of Abraham's willing consent (Antony 2011: 40). Although this dramatic passage indicates that God ultimately prevented Abraham from killing Isaac, for many, it still raises serious questions that continue to be discussed (e.g., see Kierkegaard 2006; Koller 2019). Additional objections to the Old Testament God are based on episodes such as God's extreme anger at Moses for not striking a rock exactly as commanded and God's betting with Satan about whether Job would remain faithful through suffering. It has been said that this God fits the profile of the "abusive parent" in psychology – controlling, demanding respect, requiring absolute obedience, and acting with a sense of entitlement over his children.

Twin dilemmas arise here: Old Testament passages portraying God ordering or condoning immoral acts is incompatible with the good and loving God of monotheism and with the more idealized morally perfect God of theism. The argument pattern is straightforward:

(1) The God of the Old Testament commanded (or committed) X.
(2) If God is perfectly moral and loving, God would not command (or commit) X.

Therefore,

(3) The God of the Old Testament is immoral, unloving, evil.

We can simply substitute for X any atrocity or cruelty – such as genocide, child sacrifice, vindictive anger, wagering with innocent life, and so on.

Critics also accuse the Qur'an of portraying divine evil. Since the turn of the millennium, the question of divine evil has taken on practical relevance because of the spike in religious extremism that has led to violence such as suicide bombings, beheadings, and other vicious acts. After the destruction of the World Trade Towers by Islamic terrorists on September 11, 2001, when almost 3,000 people were killed, another New Atheist Sam Harris wrote *The End of Faith: Religion, Terror, and the Future of Reason* (Harris 2005). In Islam, according to Harris, "the basic thrust of the doctrine is undeniable: convert, subjugate, or kill unbelievers; kill apostates; and conquer the world" (2005: 113). In addition to Islam, he states that Judaism and Christianity are also dangerous because their proclaimed superiority over other faiths has likewise justified holy war, ethnic cleansing, and execution. In an age of nuclear and biological weapons, warns Harris, these religions pose an existential threat to humanity.

Different responses to the underlying dilemma have been offered:

1.   Reject the God described in scriptural texts based on commonly affirmed moral principles.
2.   Advocate alternative interpretations of the scriptural texts (as nonhistorical, figurative, etc.) to emphasize deeper meanings; argue that God's revelation accommodates and was expressed via the relatively primitive moral categories and cultural contexts of Ancient Near Eastern peoples; affirm that the more morally primitive ancient texts were still part of a trajectory of divine revelation that over many centuries would fully describe God as morally good; thus, God may be portrayed as morally questionable by modern standards but in principle does no evil.
3.   Appeal to theological voluntarism, which holds that the good is whatever God commands; thus, there is no independent moral standard for evaluating God's actions.
4.   Argue that God and creatures do not share the same moral context such that God actually has no obligations toward creatures; thus, divine and human moral judgments are incommensurate.
5.   Maintain that it is possible that human moral intuitions might be mistaken or that there is no reason to believe that humans would discern any greater goods connected to ostensibly evil divine commands and actions in scripture; thus, some version of skeptical theism would apply.

Most critics endorse response (1). Although sophisticated representatives of standard theism commonly endorse (2), theistic approaches may also be found along the range of the responses (3)–(5). Thus, just as theodicies address the question of how God can be good in light of the world's evils, theistic responses to the charge of divine evil must contend that God can be good, or at least not shown to be evil, in light of troubling scriptural passages. Clearly, the problem of divine evil adds a further dimension and complexity to the overall problem of evil. For further study, see *Divine Evil? The Moral Character of the God of Abraham*, an excellent book resulting from a conference at the University of Notre Dame (Bergmann *et al.* 2011).

Analytic and Continental Approaches to Evil

Also impacting the problem of evil is a meta-philosophical disagreement about how philosophy should be conducted. Over the past several decades, Continental thinkers have critiqued analytic philosophy of religion generally and the way it approaches theodicy specifically. Philosophical analysis – with its emphasis on language, logic, and mathematics – has dominated Anglo-American professional philosophy. Its hallmarks are terminological precision and argumentative rigor analogous to that of scientific reasoning. By contrast, Continental philosophy emphasizes deconstructing common ways of thinking and speaking in order to reveal unquestioned assumptions and, perhaps, unhealthy ways of seeing the world. With roots in European thought, Continental philosophy is concerned for historical context, the conditioned nature of language, and philosophy's impact on the human condition.

The charge by Continental thinkers, then, is that theodicies (and even defenses) within analytic philosophy are dispassionate and overly abstract, whereas the problem of evil demands passionate engagement with the issues of existential response and practical action. In *The End of Philosophy of Religion*, Nick Trakakis calls for the demise of analytic philosophy of religion because its method and attitude create a "disconnection between [the] lived praxis of faith and the philosophical pursuit of wisdom" (2008: loc. 4052). Continental thinker John Caputo calls analytic philosophy an esoteric profession in which practitioners ignore life's most important issues, particularly the real-life issues represented in the problem of evil (2000: 230).

Elizabeth Burns claims that analytic theodicies are misguided in trying to make God compatible with gratuitous suffering with theodicies referring to greater goods whereas Continental philosophy insists that no possible goods can do this (2018: 152). Indeed, as Continental thinker Emmanuel Levinas wrote, the attempt to specify goods as justification for our neighbor's pain is unpardonable and "the source of all immorality" (1988: 374, 378). Unsurprisingly, a Continental approach endorses the rejection of theodicy, as we discussed in Section 5.

Burns explains that Continental thought replaces theodicy with two strategies:

> First, in order to avoid the apparent conflict between the existence of an omnipotent, benevolent deity and gratuitous suffering, they revision the concept of God, replace God with a God-like religious ultimate such as Being, Nature or Good, or claim that God is beyond Being. Secondly, they suggest several ways in which religion can help humankind to meet the challenge of evil. (2018: 153)

The first strategy replaces the personal God of monotheism with an entity or principle beyond description and thereby surrenders the theoretical activity of looking for explanations for God's ways. But this impersonal force or being is powerless against evil and at best seeks human assistance. The second strategy of engaging the practical and existential problems of evil confronts the need for action in aiding other persons and for reflection on the meaning of evil within a nonmonotheistic framework.

Since the Continental critique strikes only at the narrowest form of analytic philosophy, its wholesale rejection of analytic philosophy of religion and of analytic work on the problem of evil is extreme. After all, analysis was (and remains) key to the flourishing of philosophy of religion since the 1970s, which countered the reigning positivist paradigm that philosophy of religion is not a legitimate field because religion had been shown to be empirically, and thus conceptually, meaningless (Peterson 1998: 156–9). A great defect in the Continental critique is that it embraces one side of several familiar false dichotomies – analysis/synthesis, atomistic/contextual, objective/subjective – and thus cannot recognize the significance of analytic philosophy of religion, including its advances in theodicy. However, a valuable insight in the Continental critique is its rejection of the whole genre of greater-good theodicies.

A New Direction in Theodicy

Progress in the problem of evil will require combining the wisdom of the historic discussion with the insights of the contemporary debate. Remember Rowe's presentation of the argument (1979: 336):

(1) There exist instances of intense suffering which an omnipotent, omniscient being could have prevented without thereby losing some greater good or permitting some evil equally bad or worse.

[Factual Premise]

(2) An omniscient, wholly good being would prevent the occurrence of any intense suffering it could, unless it could not do so without thereby losing some greater good or permitting some evil equally bad or worse.

[Theological Premise]

Therefore,

(3) There does not exist an omnipotent, omniscient, wholly good being.
[Atheistic Conclusion]

Disputants on both sides typically assume that premise 2 is a necessary truth –
leaving premise 1 for theists to attack (see Peterson 2012: 178). However,
neither greater-good theodicy or skeptical theism has been able to overcome
Rowe's case for premise 1: that, as a matter of factual judgment, it is more
reasonable than not to believe that there is gratuitous evil.

It is time for a new direction of response to the argument from evil, a direction
that is tutored by insights that are unfolding in the discussions of this book. First,
we saw that traditional theodicies accent some important themes – libertarian
free will, the role of natural law, and soul-making potential – but do not provide
a convincing comprehensive answer. Second, it can be argued that Skeptical
theist defenses not only remind us that human understanding may not grasp all
goods that are related to evils but also articulate skeptical principles that risk
undercutting other reasonable beliefs about God, but such criticisms are con-
tested by many Skeptical theists (O'Connor 2013: 477; Rea 2013). Third, the
hiddenness challenge reinforces that the human sense of God's absence from the
world is often related to our frequent failures to see God-justifying reasons for
many evils. Fourth, the accusation of divine evil requires closer scrutiny of the
character of the God of monotheistic scriptures. Fifth, the critiques of theodicy
both by anti-theodicy advocates and the Continental thinkers, while overblown
and unself-critical, caution that theodicy must not gloss over the suffering of
others with pure abstractions.

With all of this as background, let us chart the needed new direction. In the
ongoing debate, a great many theists have underestimated both the strength of
the Factual Premise and the weakness of the Theological Premise. An important
first step toward a more adequate theodicy is to accept premise 1 because it is
simply more rational to believe than its denial. It is entirely reasonable to form
the judgment that the world would be better, or at least no worse, if God had
prevented a great number of evils. The monotheisms themselves actually
contain both philosophical and theological support for our powers of moral
evaluation, thereby supporting the common judgment that some evils are
gratuitous. On philosophical grounds, there is a strong presumption in favor
of the general reliability of our rational and moral powers that form such
judgments about evils. Denying the competence of our faculties invites skepticism and is itself a candidate for a pointless evil. On theological grounds,
monotheistic religions teach that our rational and moral powers, while not
infallible, are divinely given and essential to created human nature.

The second crucial step is to reject the Theological Premise as stated because it is a problematic construal of God's relation to evil. Its assumption that an omnipotent, omniscient, wholly good God would meticulously arrange the world such that all evils serve a greater good will not withstand scrutiny. What we may call the Principle of Meticulous Providence interprets the divine attributes to entail that no evil is gratuitous. As long as theists embrace Meticulous Providence, they will continue to feel pressure to explain away apparent gratuity while nontheistic critics will continue to mount the case that the gratuity is real. This endless cycle must be broken.

The way forward here is to interpret the theistic attributes in light of the relational themes available in all three major monotheisms – that is, to see God as relational and as creating the world for relationship with human beings (see Peterson *et al.* 2013: 188–9). For God to create a world with potential for genuine relationship is for God to take risks – risks that not all creatures will respond in desired ways – which is hardly meticulous providence (Hasker 2020: 317–26).

If an omnipotent, omniscient, wholly good God is relational, then this God would build structural features into the created world that make real relationship possible. Among these features are robust libertarian free will and a lawlike natural order as context for embodied personal and interpersonal life. These features, which are necessary for relationship with God and others, make gratuitous evil possible: free will makes possible nondetermined evil free choices, and the operations of nature make possible physical pain and suffering. Thus, the same structural features of the world that support the possibility of great goods are ineluctably linked to the possibility of great evils. Conversely, for God to remove or restrict the possibility of great evils within the created order is for God to remove or restrict the possibility of great goods (Peterson 1982: chap. 5). If monotheistic religion saw humanity as meant for lesser goods, then perhaps there could be more stringent limitations on human choice, but all monotheisms speak of extremely great goods pertaining to relationship with God (and others) that require a significant range of possible choices. For versions of monotheism with this perspective, this means that God is open to alternative possible outcomes in the world – that the human future is open, not closed. On this account, God does not meticulously structure the world to guarantee that all evils are necessary to greater goods – and the theist is not committed to the claim that this world is somehow better on the whole for containing all of the evil and suffering that it does.

This new direction, which includes the recognition that there are gratuitous evils, positively advances discussions of the practical, existential, and pastoral problems of evil. Progress is made on the practical problem because this view does not automatically connect evil and suffering to some greater good – and it entails that many evils are absolutely unacceptable and demand our moral energy to alleviate or eliminate them. Here, good theory paves the way for good practice, dismantling the artificial dichotomy between theory and practice. Furthermore, this view gives appropriate context to the existential problem of evil. An individual can come to grips with the meaning of his or her life with the theistic understanding that this is a good kind of world, filled with both opportunity and danger, which though flawed is still of great moral and spiritual value. To illustrate how this kind of thinking might be encouraged, consider that both the Qur'an and Sunnah teach that moral and physical evil can be reduced in practical life by improving one's spiritual condition and obeying Allah's command to resist injustice (Aslan 2001: 24–47).

Finally, the pastoral problem of evil is handled in a healthier manner since there is no need to approach the sufferer under the assumption that there is a specific reason for the suffering. The mistake of Job's friends – blaming the sufferer – can be avoided. Instead, theologians, clergy, and counselors in monotheistic traditions that accent God's relationality can communicate to the suffer that there is nondetermined contingency in the world God created – and thus that God does not specifically bring unfortunate circumstances – but that God can be particularly present with the sufferer. For example, in the New Testament, Romans 8:28 states, "God works in all things for the good of those who love him." The point is that difficult circumstances are not willed by God but that God can work with those who trust him in those difficult circumstances.

Evil and Worldview Comparison

For many theistic and nontheistic thinkers, the problem of evil is a major factor in assessing the rational credibility of theism. Although Rowe, for instance, acknowledges that the larger dialogical landscape includes other arguments both for and against the existence of God, he holds those arguments in abeyance in order to isolate the impact of evil on theism. As we know, Rowe's argument concludes that, all else held equal, gratuitous evil makes atheism more reasonable than theism. The kind of theodicy that is briefly sketched above mitigates the force of this claim by qualifying the kind of world the theistic God would (or could) create in order to explain why gratuitous evil is possible.

Furthermore, the direction in theodicy that emerges above impacts the larger argumentative context in which the problem of evil is pressed against theism. Drawing on selected items from that larger context, Rowe buttresses his atheistic conclusion with the additional claim that we are now in an "age of reason and science" in which "the idea of God no longer plays an essential, rational role in explaining the world and human existence" (2006: 87). Unfortunately, and perhaps unwittingly, Rowe here abandons his own restriction to the evidence of evil by appealing to other factors in deciding on a total view of reality. This is a tacit admission that, in the end, we must make an all-things-considered judgment about the comparative explanatory power of the worldviews that vie for our acceptance in the intellectual arena. Granting that the new proposal in theodicy diminishes the strength of the evidential argument from gratuitous evil on its own terms, we can then consider the larger worldview debate in which many other features of the world must be explained as well.

First, we must set up the worldview comparisons more completely. It has already been stated that restricted theism may anchor various defenses but is not conceptually rich enough to provide a viable theodicy, let alone to motivate the new theodicy above. The emerging thought, then, is that forms of expanded theism – Christian, Jewish, or Islamic – that affirm God's relational purposes would offer the most plausible theistic explanations of gratuitous evil. A similar point applies to what we may call "restricted atheism," which is the denial of theism but not much of a positive explanation of anything. In secular, modern Western culture, atheism generally finds its worldview home in philosophical naturalism, which explains key features of life and the world as exclusively products of nature and its processes. Naturalism as a worldview simply entails atheism. Thus, the telling worldview comparison we must make is between naturalism and any version of theism expanded to include the more complete doctrinal beliefs of some living monotheistic religion that refer to God's relational purposes for creation.

When the comparison is structured in this fashion, Rowe appears overconfident in claiming that, in addition to evil, "reason and science" tip the scales for atheism. Among the key features of the world that any worldview must explain are indeed reason and science, which theists may argue present explanatory difficulties for naturalism. Naturalism holds that the entire physical cosmos occurred by chance and thus that every feature of the cosmos is ultimately rooted in chance. However, rationality – the ability for logical reasoning and investigation – is an important phenomenon to appear within physical nature that is extremely difficult to imagine occurring in a chance universe. Furthermore, since science requires rationality, it is hard to think of science occurring in a cosmos that occurred purely by chance. Given naturalism, then, the antecedent probability of the appearance of rationality on the face of the universe is quite low – or where P is probability, R is reason, and N is naturalism:

$P(R/N)$ is low.

Likewise, given naturalism, the antecedent probability of science (S), which requires rationality, appearing in the universe is low, or:

$P(S/N)$ is low.

On these points, a worldview comparison between theism and naturalism favors theism because all theisms affirm a rational creator who wills that rational creatures come into existence. Thus, the antecedent probability of rationality on theism (T) is significantly higher than on naturalism:

$P(R/T) > P(R/N)$.

Likewise for science:

$P(S/T) > P(S/N)$.

Rationality and science only begin the list of important phenomena that every worldview must explain – such as the existence of the cosmos, consciousness, morality, personhood, an intelligible and lawlike physical order, beauty, and more.

When all these phenomena are taken together, the theistic worldview seems to have an explanatory advantage over naturalism, the typical default worldview of nontheists. Using our same comparative schema, where A represents all such key features of life and the world in aggregate, the claim is worth considering that these key features and their interconnections are more probable on theism than on naturalism. Symbolically, we get

$P(A/T) > P(A/N)$.

Of course, much more debate and discussion are needed, but the prevailing naturalism in academia and culture faces serious, though often ignored, challenges in overcoming intellectually sophisticated theistic explanations of the same phenomena. It should be noted that Paul Draper offers an evidential argument framed more explicitly at the worldview level. Draper's probabilistic case is that the random distribution of pain and pleasure in the evolutionary process makes any worldview that posits the indifference of ultimate reality toward humans (and other sentient creatures) more likely than theism (1989, 1998). Naturalism, of course, is the major nontheistic default alternative. We leave study of this type of argument to the interested reader but point out that this argument also falls to all-things-considered reasoning sketched earlier in the text (Peterson 2012: 194 n40).

Continuing our current line of thought, consider personhood and all that we commonly understand by it – such as capacity for relationship, for great moral and humane achievement, and the like. The theodicy recommended here asserts that a relational God created human beings for relational purposes that require a universe containing nondetermined contingency made possible by libertarian free will and a regular natural order. Within the framework of this kind of relational theistic world, the possibility of gratuitous evil is necessary – that is, evil that is not necessary to any greater good must be possible. In this type of world, gratuitous evils need not be actual since this type of open world can unfold in different ways; in our world, unfortunately, gratuitous evils did become actual. Nevertheless, a relational world like ours that allows nondetermined contingencies is a very good kind of world, which makes possible many goods, from simple kindness to self-sacrificial love.

None of this means that actual gratuitous evils in this world do not supply *prima facie* evidence against a theistic worldview. But it does mean that the understanding of the theistic worldview must be amplified along the lines discussed earlier to explain how the metaphysical structure of this theistic world makes gratuitous evils possible. Given the credibility of the theistic worldview in explaining other key features of the world – such as rationality, morality, and a lawlike natural order – this theistic proposal in theodicy must be taken seriously.

References

Adams, Marilyn (1991). Horrendous Evils and the Goodness of God. In Robert Adams and Marilyn Adams, eds., *The Problem of Evil*, New York: Oxford University Press, 209–21.

Adams, Marilyn (1999). *Horrendous Evils and the Goodness of God*, Ithaca, NY: Cornell University Press.

Adams, Robert M. (1987). *The Virtue of Faith and Other Essays in Philosophical Theology*, New York: Oxford University Press.

Adogbo, Michael (2010). *Comparative Historical and Interpretative Study of Religions*, Lagos: Malthouse Press.

al-Ash'arī, Abū al-Ḥasan (1940). *The Elucidation of Islam's Foundation*, Walter Klein, trans., New Haven, CT: Yale University Press.

al-Fayyumi, Saadiah ben Joseph (1988). *The Book of Theodicy*, Len Goodman, trans., New Haven, CT: Yale University Press.

al-Ghazālī, Abū Ḥāmid (1989). *The Remembrance of Death and the Afterlife*, Timothy Winter, trans., Cambridge: Islamic Texts Society.

al-Ghazālī, Abū Ḥāmid (1990). *Iḥyā' 'ulūm al-Dīn* [*Revival of Religious Sciences*] 16 parts, Cairo: Lajnat Nashr al-Thaqâfa al-Islâmiyya, 1937–38. Reprint Beirut: Dâr al-Kitâb al-'Arabî, n. d. [*c*.1990].

al-Sha'rāwī, Muḥammad Mutawallī (1995). *Good and Evil*, London: Dar Al Taqwa.

al-Sharabāṣī, Aḥmad (1956). *Fī 'ālam al-makfūfīn*, Cairo 1375/1956, vol. 1, 260–85.

al-Zamīlī, Zuhayr Muḥammad (1988). *Limādhā ja'al Allāh al-amrāḍ*, Amman 1409/1988.

Ali Shah, Zulfiqar (2012). *Anthropomorphic Depictions of God: The Concept of God in Judaic, Christian, and Islamic Traditions: Representing the Unrepresentable*, Herndon, VA: International Institute of Islamic Thought.

Antony, Louise (2011). Does God Love Us? In Michael Bergmann, Michael Murray, and Michael Rea, eds., *Divine Evil? The Moral Character of the God of Abraham*, New York: Oxford University Press, 29–46.

Aquinas, Thomas (1920). *Summa Theologica*, revised ed., Fathers of the English Dominican Province, trans., New York: Benzinger Brothers.

Arberry, Arthur John (1961). *Discourses of Rūmī*, London: John Murray.

Aslan, Adnan (2001). The Fall and the Overcoming of Evil and Suffering in Islam. In Peter Koslowski, ed., *The Origin and the Overcoming of Evil and Suffering in the World Religions*, Dordrecht: Springer, 24–47.

Augustine, Saint (1872). *The City of God*, Marcus Dods, trans., Edinburgh: T. & T. Clark.

Augustine, Saint (1887). Enchiridion. In Philip Schaff, ed., and James Shaw, trans., *Nicene and Post-Nicene Fathers*, vol. 3, Edinburgh: T&T Clark, pp. 229–276.

Augustine, Saint (1948). Enchiridion. In Whitney J. Oates, ed., and James Shaw, trans., *Basic Writings of St. Augustine* 2 vols., New York: Random House., pp. 658–732.

Augustine, Saint (1950). *City of God*, Marcus Dods, George Wilson, and J. J. Smith, trans., New York: Random House.

Augustine, Saint (1953a). The Nature of the Good. In John Burleigh, trans., *Augustine: Earlier Writings*, London: S. C. M. Press, pp. 324–348.

Augustine, Saint (1953b). On Free Will. In John Burleigh, trans., *Augustine: Earlier* Writings, London: S. C. M. Press, pp. 102–217.

Augustine, Saint (1977). *Confessions*, Maria Boulding, trans., VII.12.18, Hyde Park, NY: New City Press.

Averroes (2001). *Faith and Reason in Islam*, Ibrahim Najjar, trans., Oxford: Oneworld.

Balthasar, Hans Urs von (1994). *Theo-Drama Theological Dramatic Theory*, San Francisco, CA: Ignatius Press.

Barth, Karl (1957). *Church Dogmatics*, Edinburgh: T. & T. Clark.

Barth, Karl (1979). *Evangelical Theology: An Introduction*, Grover Foley, trans., Grand Rapids, MI: Eerdmans.

Berger, Peter L. (1967). *The Sacred Canopy*, New York: Doubleday.

Bergmann, Michael (2001). Skeptical Theism and Rowe's New Evidential Argument from Evil. *Nous* 35, no. 3, 278–96.

Bergmann, Michael, Michael Murray, and Michael Rea, eds. (2011). *Divine Evil? The Moral Character of the God of Abraham*, New York: Oxford University Press.

Blake, William (1956). The Tyger. In Louis Bedvold, Alan McKillop, Lois McIntyre, eds., *Eighteenth Century Poetry and Prose*, New York: Ronald Press.

Borowitz, Eugene (1973). *The Mask Jews Wear*, New York: Simon and Schuster.

Bowker, John (1970). *Problems of Suffering in Religions of the World*, New York: Cambridge University Press.

Braiterman, Zachary (1999). *God after Auschwitz: Tradition and Change in Post-Holocaust Jewish Thought*, Princeton, NJ: Princeton University Press.

Bray, Gerald (1983). *The Doctrine of God*, Downers Grove, IL: InterVarsity Press.

Brown, Robert McAfee (1979). Introduction. In Elie Wiesel, ed., *The Trial of God*, New York: Schocken Books, loc 42–248.

Burns, Elizabeth (2018). Continental Philosophy. In Jerome Gellman, ed., *The History of Evil from the Mid Twentieth Century to Today (1950–2010)*; Chad Meister and Charles Taliaferro, eds., *The History of Evil*, vol. 6, London: Routledge, 152–66.

Calame, Claude (2008). Greek Myth and Greek Religion. In Roger D. Woodard, ed., *The Cambridge Companion to Greek Mythology*, Cambridge: Cambridge University Press, 259–85.

Caputo, John (2000). *More Radical Hermeneutics: On Not Knowing Who We Are*, Bloomington, IN: Indiana University Press.

Chisholm, Roderick (1968). The Defeat of Good and Evil. *Proceedings and Addresses of the American Philosophical Association* 42, 21–38.

Cornman, James W. and Keith Lehrer (1970). *Philosophical Problems and Arguments: An Introduction*, New York: Macmillan.

Cragg, Kenneth (1975). *The House of Islam*, 2nd ed., Encino, CA: Dickenson.

Dawkins, Richard (2006). *The God Delusion*, New York: Bantam Press.

Diyāb, Adīb al-Nāyif (2000). Ibn Arabi on Human Freedom, Destiny and the Problem of Evil. *Al-Shajarah* 5, 24–5.

Dostoevsky, Fyodor (1976). *The Brothers Karamazov: The Constance Garnett Translation*, New York: W. W. Norton.

Dougherty, Trent and Justin McBrayer, eds. (2014). *Skeptical Theism: New Essays*, Oxford: Oxford University Press.

Draper, Paul (1989). Pain and Pleasure: An Evidential Problem for Theists. *Nous* 23, 331–50.

Draper, Paul (1998). Evolution and the Problem of Evil. In Louis P. Pojman, ed., *Philosophy of Religion: An Anthology*, 3rd ed., Belmont, CA: Wadsworth, 219–30.

Durkheim, Emile (1995). *The Elementary Forms of Religious Life*, Karen Fields, trans., New York: The Free Press.

Elman, Yaakov (1999). The Contribution of Rabbinic Thought to a Theology of Misfortune. In Shalom Carmy, ed., *Jewish Perspectives on the Experience of Suffering*, Northvale, NJ: Jason Aronson, 155–212.

Fackhenheim, Emil (1989). The 614th Commandment. In John Roth and Michael Berenbaum, eds., *Holocaust: Religious and Philosophical Implications*, New York: Paragon House, 291–5.

Flew, Antony (1955). Divine Omnipotence and Human Freedom. In Antony Flew and Alasdair MacIntyre, eds., *New Essays in Philosophical Theology*, New York: Macmillan, 144–69.

Frankenberry, Nancy (1981). Some Problems in Process Theodicy. *Religious Studies* 17, 181–4.

Frankfort, Henri, Henrietta Frankfort, John Wilson, Thorkild Jacobsen, and William Irwin (1977). *The Intellectual Adventure of Ancient Man: An Essay on Speculative Thought in the Ancient Near East*, Chicago, IL: University of Chicago Press.

Fyzee, Asaf A. A. (1942). *A Shi'ite Creed*, London: Oxford University Press.

Gaon, Saadia (2011). *The Book of Beliefs and Opinions*, Yosef Qafih, trans., Kiryat Ono: Mekhkon Mishnat ha-Rambam.

Ghaly, Mohammed (2010). *Islam and Disability*, Abingdon: Routledge.

Ghaly, Mohammed (2014). Muslim Theologians on Evil: God's Omnipotence or Justice, God's Omnipotence and Justice. In Mouhanad Khorchide, ed., *Theologie der Barmherzigkeit? Zeitgemässe Fragen und Antworten des Kalam*, Münster: Waxmann, 147–72.

Glatzer, Nahum (2002). *The Dimensions of Job*, reprint, Eugene, OR: Wipf & Stock.

Goodman, Lenn (2017). Judaism and the Problem of Evil. In Chad Meister and Paul Moser, eds., *The Cambridge Companion to the Problem of Evil*, Cambridge: Cambridge University Press, 193–209.

Griffin, David Ray (1976). *God, Power, and Evil*, Philadelphia, PA: Westminster.

Haaretz (2012). New Poll Shows Atheism on Rise, with Jews Found to Be Least Religious, August 20. www.haaretz.com/jewish/jews-least-observant-int-l-poll-finds-1.5287579

Harnack, Adolf von (1958). *History of Dogma*, Neil Buchanan, trans., vol. 1, New York: Russell & Russell.

Harris, Sam (2005). *The End of Faith: Religion, Terror, and the Future of Reason*, New York: W. W. Norton.

Hartshorne, Charles (1945). Omnipotence. In Virgilius Ferm, ed., *An Encyclopedia of Religion*, New York: Philosophical Library, 545f.

Hartshorne, Charles (1962). *The Logic of Perfection and Other Essays in Neoclassical Metaphysics*, La Salle, IL: Open Court.

Hartshorne, Charles (1984). *Omnipotence and Other Theological Mistakes*, Albany, NY: State University of New York Press.

Hasel, Gerhard (1974). The Polemic Nature of the Genesis Cosmology. *The Evangelical Quarterly* 46, 81–102.

Hasker, William (2020). God Takes Risks. In Michael Peterson and Raymond Van Arragon, eds., *Contemporary Debates in Philosophy of Religion*, 2nd ed., Oxford: Wiley-Blackwell, 317–26.

Hick, John (1978). *Evil and the God of Love*, 2nd ed., San Francisco, CA: Harper & Row.

Hoover, Jon (2007). *Ibn Taymiyya's Theodicy of Perpetual Optimism*, Leiden: Brill.

Howard-Snyder, Daniel and Adam Green (2016). Hiddenness of God. In Edward N. Zalta, ed., *The Stanford Encyclopedia of Philosophy*, Winter ed. https://plato.stanford.edu/archives/win2016/entries/divine-hiddenness/

Hume, David (1948). *Dialogues Concerning Natural Religion*, New York: Hafner Press.

Inwagen, Peter Van (2006). *The Problem of Evil: The Gifford Lectures Delivered in the University of St. Andrews in 2003*, Oxford: Clarendon.

Jackson, Sherman A. (2014). *Islam and the Problem of Black Suffering*, New York: Oxford University Press.

James, William (1961). *The Varieties of Religious Experience*, New York: Macmillan.

John Paul II (1997). *Catechism of the Catholic Church*, 2nd ed., New York: Doubleday.

Kaufman, Gordon D. (1973). *God the Problem*, Cambridge, MA: Harvard University Press.

Kaufmann, Walter (1961). *The Faith of a Heretic*, Garden City, NY: Doubleday.

Khadduri, Majid (1984). *The Islamic Conception of Justice*, Baltimore, MD: Johns Hopkins University Press.

Kierkegaard, Søren (2006). *Fear and Trembling*, C. Stephen Evans and Sylvia Walsh, eds., Cambridge: Cambridge University Press.

Koller, Aaron. (2019). Abraham Passes the Test of the Akedah But Fails as a Father. https://thetorah.com/article/abraham-passes-the-test-of-the-akedah -but-fails-as-a-father

Kramer, Samuel Noah (1981). *History Begins at Sumer: Thirty-Nine Firsts in Man's Recorded History*, 2nd ed., Philadelphia, PA: University of Pennsylvania Press.

Küng, Hans (1987). *The Incarnation of God: An Introduction to Hegel's Theological Thought as a Prolegomena to a Future Christology*, New York: Crossroad.

Lari, Sayyid Mujtaba Musavi (2003). *God and His Attributes: Lessons on Islamic Doctrine. Book One*, Hamid Algar, trans., Brooklyn Park, MN: Islamic Education Center.

Larrimore, Mark (2000). *The Problem of Evil: A Reader*, Oxford: Blackwell.

Lassley, Jennifer (2015). A Defective Covenant: Abandonment of Faith among Jewish Survivors of the Holocaust. *International Social Science Review* 90, no. 2, art. 3. http://digitalcommons.northgeorgia.edu/issr/vol90/iss2/3

Leibniz, Gottfried (1952a). Theodicy: Essays on the Goodness of God, the Freedom of Man, and the origin of Evil. In Carl Gerhardt, ed., and Eveleen Huggard, trans., *Collected Philosophical Works*, Yale University Press.

Leibniz, Gottfried (1952b). *Theodicy*, Eveleen Huggard, trans., London: Routledge & Kegan Paul.

Leibniz, Gottfried (2020). *Essays of Theodicy: The Goodness of God, the Freedom of Man, and the Origin of Evil*, Chicago, IL: OK Publishing.

Levinas, Emmanuel (1988). Useless Suffering. In Mark Larrimore, ed., and Richard Cohen, trans., *The Problem of Evil*, Oxford: Blackwell, 371–80.

Luther, Martin (2019). *The Bondage of the Will*, Henry Cole, trans., Overland Park, KS: Digireads.com.

Mackie, John L. (1955). Evil and Omnipotence. *Mind* 64, no. 254, 200–12. http://doi.org/10.1093/mind/lxiv.254.200

Madden, Edward H. and Peter H. Hare (1968). *Evil and the Concept of God*, Springfield, IL: Thomas.

Maimonides, Moses (1904). *A Guide for the Perplexed*, Michael Friedlaender, trans., 4th ed., New York: E. P. Dutton.

McBrayer, Justin and Daniel Howard-Snyder, eds. (2013). *The Blackwell Companion to the Problem of Evil*, Oxford: Wiley-Blackwell.

Meister, Chad and Paul Moser, eds. (2017). *The Cambridge Companion to the Problem of Evil*, New York: Cambridge University Press.

Melchert, Christopher (2011). God Created Adam in His Image. *Journal of Qur'anic Studies* 13, no. 1, 113–24.

Meynell, Hugo Anthony (1998). *Redirecting Philosophy: Reflections on the Nature of Knowledge from Plato to Lonergan*, London: University of Toronto Press.

Michel, Thomas (2010). God's Justice in Relation to Natural Disasters. In Ibrahim M. Abu Rabi, ed., *Theodicy and Justice in Modern Islamic Thought*, Farnham: Ashgate, 219–26.

Moltmann, Jürgen (1974). *The Crucified God: The Cross of Christ as the Foundation and Criticism of Christian Theology*, Robert Wilson and John Bowden, trans., London: SCM Press.

Moltmann, Jurgen (2015). *The Crucified God*, Minneapolis: Fortress Press.

Murray, Michael (2003). Deus Absconditus. In Dan Howard-Snyder and Paul Moser, eds., *Divine Hiddenness: New Essays*, Cambridge: Cambridge University Press, kindle ed., loc. 1085–1430.

O'Connor, Daniel and Francis Oakley (1969). *Creation: The Impact of an Idea*, New York: Scribner.

O'Connor, David (2013). *The Blackwell Companion to the Problem of Evil*, Oxford: Wiley-Blackwell.

Ormsby, Eric (1984). *Theodicy in Islamic Thought: The Dispute Over Al-Ghazali's Best of All Possible Worlds*, Princeton, NJ: Princeton University Press.

Otten, Henry J. (1985). *The Ahmadiyya Doctrine of God*, Hyderabad: Henry Martin Institute of Islamic Studies.

Pannenberg, Wolfhart (1973). *Basic Questions in Theology*, vol. 1, London: SCM Press.

Pascal, Blaise (1966). *Pensees*, Baltimore, MD: Penguin.

Peterson, Michael L. (1982). *Evil and the Christian God*, Grand Rapids, MI: Baker.

Peterson, Michael L. (1987). God and Evil in Process Theodicy. In Ronald Nash, ed., *Process Theology*, Grand Rapids, MI: Baker Book House, 123.

Peterson, Michael L. (1998). A Long and Faithful Journey. *Faith and Philosophy* 15, no. 2, 156–9. http://doi.org/10.5840/faithphil199815223

Peterson, Michael L. (2008). C. S. Lewis on the Necessity of Gratuitous Evil. In David Baggett, Gary Habermas, and Jerry Walls, eds., *Truth, Goodness, and Beauty: C. S. Lewis as Philosopher*, Downers Grove, IL: Intervarsity Press, 175–92.

Peterson, Michael L. (2012). Christian Theism and the Evidential Argument from Evil. In David Werther and Mark Linville, eds., *Philosophy and the Christian Worldview: Analysis, Assessment and Development*, New York: Continuum, kindle ed., 175–274.

Peterson, Michael L. (2017). *The Problem of Evil: Selected Readings*, Notre Dame, IN: University of Notre Dame Press.

Peterson, Michael, William Hasker, Bruce Reichenbach, and David Basinger (2013). *Reason & Religious Belief: An Introduction to the Philosophy of Religion*, 5th ed., New York: Oxford University Press.

Pinnock, Clark (1994). *The Openness of God: A Biblical Challenge to the Traditional Understanding of God*, Downers Grove, IL: InterVarsity Press.

Plantinga, Alvin (1967). *God and Other Minds; a Study in the Rational Justification of Belief in God*, Ithaca, NY: Cornell University Press.

Plantinga, Alvin (1979). The Probabilistic Argument from Evil. *Philosophical Studies* 35, no. 1, 1–53. http://doi.org/10.1007/bf00354802

Plantinga, Alvin (1985). Self-Profile. In James Tomberlin and Peter Van Inwagen, eds., *Profiles Volume Alvin Plantinga*, Dordrecht: D. Reidel, 49.

Plantinga, Alvin (2000). *Warranted Christian Belief*, New York: Oxford University Press.

Plantinga, Alvin (2004). Supralapsarianism, or "O Felix Culpa." In Peter Van Inwagen, ed., *Christian Faith and the Problem of Evil*, Grand Rapids, MI: Eerdmans, 1–25.

Plantinga, Alvin (2008). *God, Freedom and Evil*, Grand Rapids, MI: William B. Eerdmans, kindle ed.

Rahman, Fazlur (2000). *Revival and Reform in Islam: A Study of Islamic Fundamentalism*, Ebrahim Moosa, ed., Oxford: Oxford University Press.

Rea, Michael (2013). The "Too-Much-Skepticism" Objection. In Justin McBrayer and Daniel Howard-Snyder, eds., *The Blackwell Companion to Skeptical Theism*, Oxford: Wiley-Blackwell, 486–506.

Rodd, Cyril (2001). *Glimpses of a Strange Land: Studies in Old Testament Ethics*, Edinburgh: T. & T. Clark.

Rouzati, Nasrin (2018). Evil and Human Suffering in Islamic Thought: Towards a Mystical Theodicy. *Religions* 9, no. 2, 3. http://doi.org/10.3390/rel9020047

Rowe, William (1979). The Problem of Evil and Some Varieties of Atheism. *American Philosophical Quarterly* 16, 335–41.

Rowe, William (1989). Evil and Theodicy. *Philosophical Topics* 16, 119–32.

Rowe, William (1998). Atheism. In Edward Craig, ed., *Routledge Encyclopedia of Philosophy*, vol. 1, London: Routledge, 530–34.

Rowe, William (2001). Skeptical Theism: A Response to Bergmann. *Nous* 35, no. 2, 212–39. http://doi.org/10.1111/0029-4624.00298

Rowe, William (2006). Friendly Atheism, Skeptical Theism, and the Problem of Evil. *International Journal for Philosophy of Religion* 59, 87.

Russell, Bruce (1989). The Persistent Problem of Evil. *Faith and Philosophy* 6, no. 2, 121–39. http://doi.org/10.5840/faithphil19896221

Salmon, Wesley C. (1978). Religion and Science: A New Look at Hume's Dialogues. *Philosophical Studies* 33, no. 2, 143–76. http://doi.org/10.1007/bf00571884

Sanders, John (1994). Historical Considerations. In Clark Pinnock, Richard Rice, John Sanders, William Hasker, David Basinger, eds., *The Openness of God: A Biblical Challenge to the Traditional Understandings of God*, Downers Grove, IL: InterVarsity, 59–100.

Sarot, Marcel (1992). *God, Passibility and Corporeality*, Kampen: Kok Pharos.

Schellenberg, John (1993). *Divine Hiddenness and Human Reason*, Ithaca, NY: Cornell University Press.

Schleiermacher, Friedrich (1928). *The Christian Faith*, Edinburgh: T. & T. Clark.

Shatz, David (2013). On Constructing a Jewish Theodicy. In *The Blackwell Companion to the Problem of Evil*, Oxford: Wiley-Blackwell, 309–25.

Sherwin, Bryon (1988). Theodicy. In Arthur Cohen and Paul Mendes-Flohr, eds., *Contemporary Jewish Religious Thought: Original Essays on Critical Concepts, Movements, and Beliefs*, New York: The Free Press, 959–70.

Stewart, Melville (1993). *The Greater-Good Defense*, New York: St. Martin's.

Surin, Kenneth (1986). *Theology and the Problem of Evil*, Oxford: Blackwell.

Swinburne, Richard (2004). *The Existence of God*, Oxford: Clarendon.

Tertullian (1722). *Prescriptions against the Heretics*, Joseph Betty, trans., Oxford: Oxford University Press.

Tilley, Terrence (1991). *The Evils of Theodicy*, Washington, DC: Georgetown University Press.

Tippett, Krista and Elie Wiesel (2012). The Tragedy of the Believer (Interview), November 20, 2003. https://onbeing.org/programs/elie-wiesel-the-tragedy-of-the-believer/#transcript

Trakakis, Nick (2008). *The End of Philosophy of Religion*, London: Bloomsbury.

Trakakis, Nick (2017). Anti-Theodicy. In Chad Meister and Paul Moser, eds., *The Cambridge Companion to the Problem of Evil*, Cambridge: Cambridge University Press, 124–46.

Tsevat, Matitiahu (1966). The Meaning of the Book of Job. *Hebrew Union College Annual* 37.

Waugh, Earle (1999). *The Islamic Tradition: Religious Beliefs and Healthcare Decisions*, Chicago, IL: The Park Ridge Center for the Study of Health, Faith, and Ethics.

Weiss-Halivni, David (1998). *The Book and the Sword: A Life of Learning in the Shadow of the Sword*, Abingdon: Routledge.

Wettstein, Howard (1999). Against Theodicy. *The Proceedings of the Twentieth World Congress of Philosophy* 4, 115–25.

Whitehead, Alfred North (1926). *Religion in the Making*, New York: Macmillan.

Whitehead, Alfred North (1929). *Process and Reality*, New York: Macmillan.

Wiesel, Elie. (1958). *Night*, New York: Hill and Wang.

Winter, Timothy (2017). Islam and the Problem of Evil. In Chad Meister and Paul Moser, eds., *The Cambridge Companion to the Problem of Evil*, Cambridge: Cambridge University Press, 230–48.

Wright, Nicholas T. (2012). *Evil and the Justice of God*, Downers Grove, IL: InterVarsity Press.

Wykstra, Stephen (1984). The Humean Obstacle to Evidential Arguments from Suffering: On Avoiding the Evils of Appearance. *International Journal for Philosophy of Religion* 16, 73–93.

Acknowledgments

I would like to thank several persons who helped greatly in the preparation of this Element. Mara Eller made helpful suggestions on prose style. Nicholas Grounds, my research assistant during the writing of this volume, helped get the manuscript ready for publication. Following Nick, my research assistants Emily Mahoney and Evan Drysdale helped perfect the proofs.

Cambridge Elements $\equiv$

Religion and Monotheism

Paul K. Moser

Loyola University Chicago

Paul K. Moser is Professor of Philosophy at Loyola University Chicago. He is the author of *Understanding Religious Experience; The God Relationship; The Elusive God* (winner of national book award from the Jesuit Honor Society); *The Evidence for God; The Severity of God; Knowledge and Evidence* (all Cambridge University Press); and *Philosophy after Objectivity* (Oxford University Press); coauthor of *Theory of Knowledge* (Oxford University Press); editor of *Jesus and Philosophy* (Cambridge University Press) and *The Oxford Handbook of Epistemology* (Oxford University Press); coeditor of *The Wisdom of the Christian Faith (*Cambridge University Press). He is the coeditor with Chad Meister of the book series *Cambridge Studies in Religion, Philosophy, and Society.*

Chad Meister

Bethel University

Chad Meister is Professor of Philosophy and Theology and Department Chair at Bethel College. He is the author of *Introducing Philosophy of Religion* (Routledge, 2009), *Christian Thought: A Historical Introduction*, 2nd edition (Routledge, 2017), and *Evil: A Guide for the Perplexed*, 2nd edition (Bloomsbury, 2018). He has edited or coedited the following: *The Oxford Handbook of Religious Diversity* (Oxford University Press, 2010), *Debating Christian Theism* (Oxford University Press, 2011), with Paul Moser, *The Cambridge Companion to the Problem of Evil* (Cambridge University Press, 2017), and with Charles Taliaferro, *The History of Evil* (Routledge 2018, in six volumes).

About the Series

This Cambridge Element series publishes original concise volumes on monotheism and its significance. Monotheism has occupied inquirers since the time of the Biblical patriarch, and it continues to attract interdisciplinary academic work today. Engaging, current, and concise, the Elements benefit teachers, researched, and advanced students in religious studies, Biblical studies, theology, philosophy of religion, and related fields.

Cambridge Elements ⹀

Religion and Monotheism

Elements in the Series

A full series listing is available at: www.cambridge.org/er&m